The Chronicles of Narnia
The Lion, the Witch and the Wardrobe

by C. S. Lewis

Level 3
(1600-word)

Adapted by Raina Ruth Nakamura

IBC パブリッシング

はじめに

　ラダーシリーズは、「はしご（ladder）」を使って一歩一歩上を目指すように、学習者の実力に合わせ、無理なくステップアップできるよう開発された英文リーダーのシリーズです。

　リーディング力をつけるためには、繰り返したくさん読むこと、いわゆる「多読」がもっとも効果的な学習法であると言われています。多読では、「1. 速く 2. 訳さず英語のまま 3. なるべく辞書を使わず」に読むことが大切です。スピードを計るなど、速く読むよう心がけましょう（たとえば TOEIC® テストの音声スピードはおよそ 1 分間に 150語です）。そして一語ずつ訳すのではなく、英語を英語のまま理解するくせをつけるようにします。こうして読み続けるうちに語感がついてきて、だんだんと英語が理解できるようになるのです。まずは、ラダーシリーズの中からあなたのレベルに合った本を選び、少しずつ英文に慣れ親しんでください。たくさんの本を手にとるうちに、英文書がすらすら読めるようになってくるはずです。

《本シリーズの特徴》

- 中学校レベルから中級者レベルまで5段階に分かれています。自分に合ったレベルからスタートしてください。
- クラシックから現代文学、ノンフィクション、ビジネスと幅広いジャンルを扱っています。あなたの興味に合わせてタイトルを選べます。
- 巻末のワードリストで、いつでもどこでも単語の意味を確認できます。レベル1、2では、文中の全ての単語が、レベル3以上は中学校レベル外の単語が掲載されています。
- カバーにヘッドホーンマークのついているタイトルは、オーディオ・サポートがあります。ウェブから購入／ダウンロードし、リスニング教材としても併用できます。

《使用語彙について》

レベル1：中学校で学習する単語約1000語

レベル2：レベル1の単語＋使用頻度の高い単語約300語

レベル3：レベル1の単語＋使用頻度の高い単語約600語

レベル4：レベル1の単語＋使用頻度の高い単語約1000語

レベル5：語彙制限なし

CONTENTS

The Chronicles of Narnia

The Lion, the Witch and the Wardrobe

［主な登場人物］

スーザン Susan：4人きょうだいの長女。清楚でおとなしく、弟、妹の世話をする。サンタクロースから「弓矢とホーン」が与えられる。

ピーター Peter：4人きょうだいの長男で、弟のエドマンドを時に叱ることもある。サンタクロースから「盾と剣」をもらい、白の魔女と戦う。

エドマンド Edmund：4人きょうだいの次男。白い魔女に騙されて、一度はきょうだいを裏切るが、最後にはきょうだいの窮地を救う活躍をする。

ルーシー Lucy：4人きょうだいの末っ子。最初に洋服だんすを通ってナルニア国にやってくる冒険好きな無邪気な女の子。「どんな傷も治せる液体とナイフ」をサンタクロースからもらう。

教授 The Professor：4人きょうだいが戦争の間、ロンドンを離れて暮らした家の持ち主。

白の魔女 The White Witch：ナルニア国を1年中冬にして、決してクリスマスが来ないようにした。タムナスに人間に出会ったら連れてくるようにと命じた。

アスラン Aslan：森の王のライオン。ナルニア国を魔女から救うために戻ってきた。

ビーバー夫妻 Mr. Beaver/Mrs. Beaver：タムナスに頼まれて、4人きょうだいを助ける。

タムナス Tumnus：ギリシャ神話やローマ神話に登場する半人半獣の神話の生き物。ルーシーが初めにあったナルニア国の住人。

小人 dwarf：白の女王の乗るソリの御者。

読みはじめる前に

　この本で使われている用語です。わからない語は巻末のワードリストで確認しましょう。

- ☐ armor
- ☐ awe
- ☐ batty
- ☐ betray
- ☐ bungle
- ☐ dearie
- ☐ disobey
- ☐ explore
- ☐ faun
- ☐ fearsome
- ☐ genie
- ☐ holly
- ☐ kidnap
- ☐ liar
- ☐ Majesty
- ☐ mean
- ☐ mine
- ☐ myth
- ☐ nightmare
- ☐ reindeer
- ☐ satyr
- ☐ sleigh
- ☐ statue
- ☐ traitor
- ☐ treason
- ☐ wand
- ☐ whisker

【Turkish Delight について】

　第4章に登場する Turkish Delight は、トルコ語ではロクム（Lokum）と呼ばれるトルコ発祥の菓子です。日本ではあまり知られていませんが、砂糖、デンプン、果物のエッセンス、ナッツなどを煮詰めて固めたもので、通常は細長い形に切り分けられています。甘くて柔らかく、風味豊かな果物の香りが特徴的で、世界中で愛されているお菓子です。

　白の魔女はエドマンドに Turkish Delight を与え、そのおいしさにエドマンドは彼女に協力するようになってしまいます。このシーンは、欲望にとらわれることがどれほど危険であるかを、象徴的に表現する重要なエピソードとして知られています。

My Dear Lucy,

I wrote this story for you, but when I began it, I did not remember that girls grow up faster than books can be written. So, now that the book is finished, you are too old for fairy tales. But someday I hope you start reading fairy tales again. When that day comes, you can take this book from the shelf, dust it off, and read it. Then, please tell me what you think of it. Of course, I will probably be too old to hear or understand you, but I will always be your loving Godfather.

C. S. Lewis

Chapter One

Lucy Looks into a Wardrobe

Once there were four children named Peter, Susan, Edmund and Lucy. This story is about what happened when they left London because of the war. Their parents sent them on a train to the countryside to live with a professor in his great, big house. The Professor was very old and had white hair all over his face. When they met him, Lucy was a bit scared and Edmund thought he looked funny. But he was a kind man and told them they could go anywhere in the house. When it was close to bedtime on the first night, the children gathered in the girls' room.

"This is going to be great," said Peter. "There are woods and mountains and a small river around here. We can go exploring tomorrow."

Suddenly, there was a strange sound and Lucy said, "What's that?" She wasn't used to being in such a large house.

"It's only an owl, silly," said Edmund.

"There must be lots of birds around here," said Peter.

"And badgers?" asked Lucy.

"Yes, and foxes," said Peter.

"Rabbits, too," added Susan.

They were looking forward to exploring, but the next day it was raining.

"It would rain on our first day, of course," said Edmund unhappily. "Nothing to do."

"There's lots to do," said Peter. "I'm going to look in all the rooms."

The other children went with Peter and that is how their adventure in Narnia began.

First, they went into a room that was painted all green. Next, they found a room that had a suit of armor and after that, there was a huge room full of books. Then they came to a room that was empty except for a large wardrobe in the corner. It was the type of wardrobe with mirrors on the front doors. Peter, Susan and Edmund went to see what was in the rooms down the hall, but Lucy wanted to look inside the wardrobe.

She opened the door and saw long fur coats hanging inside. Lucy loved the feel of fur, so she stepped inside. She closed the door most of the way, but not all the way. Everybody knows it is silly to close

a wardrobe door all the way. It was very dark inside the wardrobe and she put her hands out in front of her. She found another row of coats behind the first row. Soon, she felt something cold and wet on her hands. And instead of soft fur on her cheeks, she felt the hard and scratchy branches of trees. She looked down and saw snow under her feet. A moment later she was outside with trees all around and snowflakes falling on her face. She was a little scared but also felt excited. She looked back to see the light in the room where the wardrobe was.

"I can go back there any time," she thought to herself.

She started walking toward a light she saw

ahead. Soon she saw a lamppost in the middle of the trees.

"That's strange," she thought and then she heard some footsteps behind her. She turned around to see a very unusual person standing under the lamppost. He was a Faun. He had the body of a man and the legs of a goat. He had a strange but kind-looking face and two horns coming out of his curly hair on each side of his head. He was carrying an umbrella to keep the snow off, and his neck was wrapped with a red muffler.

When he saw Lucy, he cried out, "Oh, my goodness!"

Chapter Two

What Lucy Found There

"Good evening," said Lucy.

The Faun was so surprised that he couldn't speak for a moment. Finally, he said, "Good evening. Uh, I don't mean to be rude, but are you a, a human?"

"Of course I am," Lucy replied.

"And you're a girl?" asked the Faun.

"Yes, silly. I'm a human girl. Haven't you ever seen one before?"

The Faun thought for a moment and said, "No, there are no humans in Narnia."

"Narnia?" Lucy asked. "Is that what this place is called?"

"Of course," said the Faun. "Haven't you heard of Narnia?"

"Well, no, I haven't," replied Lucy.

"Then let me welcome you to Narnia. My

name is Tumnus."

"It's very nice to meet you, Mr. Tumnus," Lucy said politely.

"May I ask, Human Girl Lucy, how you came to Narnia?"

"Well, I came through the wardrobe in the extra room."

"Oh, dear. Oh, dear." Mr. Tumnus was shaking his head. "I really wished I had studied harder in geography class. I don't know about countries like War Drobe and Ex Traroom."

"No, no," Lucy said, nearly laughing. "Those aren't countries. There's a room in a house. It's back there." She pointed toward the way she came, but she couldn't see anything except trees and snow. "I mean, I think it's that way."

She was about to say more, but the Faun looked around as if he was scared.

"Maybe we'd better not talk here. Let's go to my house and have some tea."

Lucy wasn't sure she should go, but the Faun said it was only a short way and he promised a warm fire and cake and toast and sardines. She was cold and hungry, so she agreed. She took his arm and walked with him under his umbrella, like they were old friends.

After a few minutes of walking through the snow, the Faun said, "We're here."

He walked into a hole in a large rock. Lucy followed him and found herself in a cave. As the Faun lit a fire, Lucy looked around at the nice, clean cave. There was a carpet on the floor and a table with two chairs in the middle of the room. Many books and some pictures sat on a bookshelf. While Mr. Tumnus set the table with tea things, Lucy read some of the book titles, like *Nymphs and Their Ways* and *Is Man a Myth?*

Soon, tea was ready and when Lucy sat down, she was very glad to rest her short legs. Mr. Tumnus served the tea, along with toast and sardines, toast with butter, and toast with honey. Then there was a delicious cake. Lucy ate all this while listening to the Faun's stories about Narnia. He told her about the magical creatures who lived in the trees. There was a white deer who gave you wishes. There were short people who dug in mines and tree spirits who liked to dance with the Fauns. And in the summer, the god of wine named Bacchus would come and turn the rivers into wine.

"But, of course, we don't go out much now. It's winter all the time with no Christmas, so there is no more fun."

Mr. Tumnus looked very sad as he said this. To make himself happier, he picked up a small flute and began to play. Lucy enjoyed the music very much. She wanted to dance, laugh, cry and go to sleep all at the same time.

Finally, she said, "Mr. Tumnus, I do like your music very much. But I should go home now."

When Lucy said this, the Faun put down his flute and started crying.

"Don't worry," said Lucy. "I'll come visit you again."

But Mr. Tumnus only cried harder. He put his hands over his face and began to yell with sadness.

"Oh, I'm sorry. It's just that I, I..." He was crying so hard now that he could not speak.

Lucy went to his side and patted him on the back, like he was a child.

"It's ok, Mr. Faun. Don't cry." She handed

him her handkerchief, which he used until it was very, very wet.

Finally, Lucy had had enough. She shook Mr. Tumnus and yelled, "Do stop now! You're a big Faun! What are you crying about?"

"Oh, dear Lucy," Mr. Tumnus said, still crying. "I'm crying because I'm such a bad Faun. There has never been a worse Faun since the beginning of the world."

"What do you mean? I don't think you're a bad Faun. You are the nicest Faun I've ever met." Lucy hoped he wouldn't remember that he was the only Faun she had ever met.

"You don't know. It's terrible. My dear father," he looked over at a picture of an old Faun sitting on the bookshelf, "he would never have done such a bad thing."

"What bad thing have you done?" Lucy asked. She was beginning to feel scared but she didn't know why.

"I've taken money from the White Witch. She paid me to, uh, to *kidnap* you."

Now Lucy was very scared. "Who is this White Witch?"

"She's the one who has made it always winter and never Christmas in Narnia. She controls all the magic now. She told me that if I ever met humans in Narnia, I should kidnap them for her. So I invited you here and was waiting for you to go to sleep. Then I was planning to go to her house and tell her about you."

Lucy felt her skin go cold. But she couldn't believe Mr. Tumnus would put her in danger.

"But you won't do that, will you, Mr. Tumnus? You have to let me go home," said Lucy. "Please."

"Of course I will. But we must hurry back to the lamppost."

They left quickly and quietly because Mr. Tumnus said even the trees were watching for humans. And they would tell the White Witch. Soon, they came to the lamppost.

"Do you know the way back to War Drobe from here?" the Faun asked.

"Yes, I do," Lucy replied.

"Then go quickly. And please, please forgive me for what I did."

"Of course," Lucy said as she shook his hand. "And keep my handkerchief to remember me!"

15

Lucy ran toward the wardrobe door as quickly as her short legs would go.

"I hope you don't get in trouble because of me," she called as she was running.

Soon she saw the fur coats, and she pushed her way through them. When she stepped out of the front door of the wardrobe, she could see it was still raining outside. She heard her brothers and sister out in the hall.

She yelled excitedly, "I'm ok. I'm back!"

Chapter Three

Edmund and the Wardrobe

When she saw Peter and Susan and Edmund, she said, "I'm sorry I was gone a long time. I hope you weren't worried."

Susan looked strangely at her. "What are you talking about, Lucy?" she asked.

"I've been gone for hours. Haven't you been looking for me?"

"Oh, Lu, you've been hiding and no one was looking for you," Peter said, thinking Lucy had been playing hide and seek. "Too bad. I guess you'll have to hide longer next time."

"But, I was in a different place and there was a forest and snow and..." Lucy spoke quickly and soon lost her breath.

"She's batty!" said Edmund, pointing to his head.

"Come on now, Lucy," said Susan kindly.

"We just came out of that room a few minutes ago and we saw you in there then."

Lucy was so confused. She tried to explain.

"But it's a magic wardrobe! There's a whole different country on the other side. And there's a Faun, Mr. Tumnus. I had tea with him. He said it's called Narnia, this place. And there's a Witch." She stopped suddenly. "Ok, if you don't believe me, come and see for yourself."

So all the children went to the extra room with the wardrobe. Susan opened the door and pushed the coats back.

"It looks like a normal wardrobe to me," she said.

Peter stepped inside and knocked on the back wall. "See, Lucy? Solid wood back here." Lucy looked in herself and saw that they were right.

Peter said, "You were just having a bit of fun, weren't you, Lu? Making up a grand story about Narnia."

"But I'm telling the truth. It was all different a few moments ago. Honest," she said. Then, she started crying because she was a truthful girl and it hurt her that no one believed her.

During the next few days, Lucy was very unhappy. The weather was fine and the children spent their time swimming, fishing and climbing trees. But Lucy could not have any fun. Edmund teased Lucy about finding new countries in all the other cupboards and closets in the house. He made her feel worse.

On one rainy afternoon the following week, the children decided to play hide and seek. Susan was 'it' and the other children went to find hiding places while she counted to 20. Lucy didn't want to hide in the wardrobe, but she wanted to look inside when the others weren't with her, just to check. She walked into the extra room and went to the wardrobe. She opened the door and saw the coats. But then she heard someone coming in the hall. She thought it was Susan, so she stepped inside the wardrobe, leaving the door open a bit, of course.

The person coming in the hall was not Susan, but Edmund. He decided to hide in the wardrobe. He opened the door, got in, and shut the door behind him. It was very dark and he could feel the coats as he walked toward the back, but Lucy was not there.

He called out, "Lucy! Lu! I know you're in here!"

Strangely, his voice sounded like he was outside, not in a wardrobe. Now Edmund got scared and suddenly, he felt very cold. A few steps later, he saw light and he walked toward it, thinking the door to the wardrobe had opened by itself. But instead of stepping into the extra room, Edmund stepped into a forest of trees covered with snow. There was no sound and the sun was just coming up. He was cold and a bit unhappy now that he discovered Lucy had been right about Narnia.

Edmund didn't like saying he was wrong, but he was scared in this strange place, so he called out again, "Say, Lucy, I see you were right! Come out now, please!" But there was no answer.

"Just like a girl," Edmund thought. "She

doesn't want to hear me say I'm sorry."

He was getting colder and colder and wanted to go back to the warm house. He turned to leave but then he heard some bells. The bell sound got closer and soon he saw a sleigh coming toward him through the snow. It was pulled by two white reindeer that were the size of ponies. In the driver's seat sat a dwarf covered in white fur. He had a red hat and a long beard that went down to his knees. Behind the dwarf was the tallest woman Edmund had ever seen. Her skin was pure white, like sugar, and she had very red lips. She had a golden crown on her head and held a wand in her right hand.

When she saw Edmund, she yelled "Stop!" and the dwarf pulled the rope on the reindeer very hard.

The tall woman looked at Edmund with hard eyes and said, "What, I ask, are you?"

"I'm, I'm Edmund," said Edmund in a small voice. The lady was quite scary looking.

"I am the Queen, you know. You should speak to me with more respect."

"Oh, I'm sorry, your Majesty. I didn't know."

"How could you not know? I am the Queen of Narnia!" the lady yelled. "But I have to ask you again. What are you?"

By this time, Edmund was so confused and so cold and so scared that he didn't know what to say.

"Please, your Majesty. I'm at school, I mean, not right now because it's the summer holiday."

Chapter Four

Turkish Delight

The queen cried loudly again, "Answer my question, fool. What are you? A dwarf that has grown tall?"

"No," said Edmund, "I'm just a boy."

The Queen looked interested now. "A boy, a human boy?"

"Yes, your Majesty."

"And how did you come to Narnia?" asked the Queen.

"I came through a door, uh, a wardrobe door. I don't really know how..."

The Queen nodded her head. "Yes, I have heard of these doors from the human world."

She stood up and Edmund saw that she was even taller than he had thought.

"You look cold, my poor boy," she said in a kind way. "Come sit here with me and I will share my fur blanket."

He didn't really want to sit next to her, but he knew he shouldn't disobey her and he was terribly cold. So Edmund got into the sleigh, and the Queen wrapped her fur blanket around him.

"Would you like a hot drink?" she asked politely.

When Edmund nodded yes, the Queen opened a small copper bottle and poured one drop onto the snow. As it touched the snow, a beautiful cup with something warm inside appeared. The dwarf picked it up and gave it to Edmund. Edmund drank the whole thing and felt better right away.

Then the Queen asked him what he liked best to eat.

"Turkish Delight, your Majesty," said Edmund quickly.

The Queen poured another drop from her copper bottle and now there was a round metal box with a green ribbon in the snow. When Edmund opened it, he saw many pieces of his favorite candy, Turkish Delight, with plenty of powdered sugar on top. He started putting piece after piece into his mouth. Now he was quite warm and comfortable.

While he ate and drank, the Queen asked him questions. She asked him how many brothers and sisters he had. He told her that one of his sisters had already visited Narnia and had met a Faun here. The Queen asked a few times how many brothers and sisters he had. He always answered 'three.'

Finally, the Turkish Delight was gone and Edmund really wanted some more. Of course, he did not know that he had eaten magical Turkish Delight, which made him want more and more until he believed he could not live without having it.

The Queen said, "I would like to meet your brother and sisters. Bring them to me."

"If I do that, will I be able to have more

Turkish delight?" asked Edmund.

The Queen said, "Of course you will. In my house, there are whole rooms filled with Turkish Delight. And, since I have no children, I will make you a prince of Narnia. You will someday be King."

Edmund thought this sounded very nice. He wanted to be King so he would be higher than Peter. But more than anything right then, Edmund wanted more Turkish Delight. When he asked politely for more, the Queen told him that her magic only works once outside. When he came to her house, she promised she would give him as much Turkish Delight as he wanted. That is, if he brought his brother and sisters with him.

"But how will I know where you live?" he asked.

The Queen answered by pointing her wand behind them.

"Do you see those two hills? I live between them. Just follow this path and you will find it."

Edmund was sorry to get off of the sleigh and to leave the empty box of Turkish Delight. But he remembered what the Queen said about rooms full of Turkish Delight at her house, and he promised he would come back with Peter, Susan and Lucy as soon as possible.

"That is good. I would be very angry with you if you came alone," the Queen said. "And don't tell your brother and sisters about me. It will be fun to keep it a secret from them, won't it?"

"I suppose so," said Edmund, still sad about the Turkish Delight.

The Queen made a sign for the dwarf to start the sleigh and she called to Edmund as it pulled away. "Next time! Next time! Don't forget. Come soon."

Edmund watched the sleigh slide off through the trees, and then he heard someone call his name. It was Lucy.

"Oh, Edmund. You're here! Isn't it wonderful?" she cried.

"Yes, yes. You were right about the magic wardrobe and Narnia. I will say sorry if that's what you want. But I've been looking for you. Where have you been?"

Edmund sounded mean and his face was red,

but Lucy was so happy to see him that she didn't notice. She spoke quickly about her second time in Narnia.

"I had lunch with Mr. Tumnus and he's quite well. The White Witch has not done anything to him for letting me go."

"Who's the White Witch?" Edmund asked.

"Oh, she's a terrible person who controls Narnia. Mr. Tumnus told me she's the one who made it winter all the time here, and without Christmas! She can turn people and animals into stone. All the creatures of this land hate her. And she rides a sleigh pulled by reindeer."

As Lucy talked, Edmund felt sicker and sicker inside. Did he really make friends with a dangerous witch? But, he still wanted Turkish Delight more than anything.

"You can't believe everything a Faun says. Everyone knows that," Edmund said. "Let's not stand here any longer. It's cold. I want to go home."

"Good idea. Oh, Edmund, when Susan and Peter hear you have been to Narnia too, they have to believe me. How fun!"

As they walked toward home, Edmund was not sure it would be very much fun. Lucy was on the side of the Faun and the other animals and he was sure Peter and Susan would also choose that side. But he was mostly on the other side, the Witch's side. Could he keep his promise to the Witch secret?

Soon they were through the trees and in the middle of the coats in the wardrobe. They stepped out into the extra room and Lucy turned to look at Edmund.

"Why, Edmund! You don't look well at all. What's the matter?" she asked.

"It's nothing. I'm all right," Edmund lied.

But Lucy believed him and went to find the others.

"What wonderful adventures we will have all together in Narnia now!" she yelled as she ran out of the room.

Chapter Five

Back on This Side of the Door

When Lucy and Edmund finally found Peter and Susan, Lucy began talking quickly.

"It's true, it's true. It's really true! Edmund has been to Narnia, too. He went through the wardrobe just like I said. Tell them, Edmund. Tell them."

Now comes one of the most disappointing parts of the story. Edmund was feeling sick from eating too much Turkish Delight. And he was feeling annoyed because Lucy had been right about Narnia. So when both Peter and Susan looked at him and said, "Yes, tell us, Ed," he couldn't stand it.

He looked down at Lucy as if he was a lot older (though he was only a bit older) and said with a laugh, "Oh, Lucy and I have played a game about a country in the wardrobe. It was just for fun. Really, there's nothing there."

When Lucy heard these words, she ran out of the room.

"What's the matter with her? She's always—" Edmund began.

But Peter yelled at Edmund. "Shut up! You have been terrible to Lucy about this Narnia matter. I think you played along with her today just to be mean."

"But, but, it isn't real!" Edmund said, surprised.

"I know it isn't. But we can all see that something's not right with Lucy. When we came here, she began making up these stories. You're not helping by teasing her about it one day and going along with it the next day. You're being a monster."

Edmund started to say something, but Susan stopped him. "Please stop fighting, you two. We need to find Lucy."

When they found Lucy later, they could see that she had been crying. But she told them she didn't care if they believed her or not.

"Write to mother. Talk to the Professor. Do

anything you want," Lucy said. "There really is a faun in there. I wish I lived with him instead of you."

Peter and Susan decided to speak with the Professor about Lucy. The next day they went to his study. He welcomed them in and they all sat down. Peter began to talk about Lucy and Susan added some details. The Professor listened to the whole story without stopping them.

When they were finished talking, he asked, "How do you know that your sister's story isn't true?"

Peter and Susan were surprised. They both started to speak.

"But a magical world?" asked Susan.

"Through the wardrobe?" asked Peter.

Then the Professor asked another question. "Has Lucy always told the truth before?"

The two children agreed that she had always been honest.

"Well, I don't know about magical wardrobes and talking animals. I just know that if you have trusted your sister up to now, maybe you should trust her about this also."

"So you don't think she's, she's..." Peter made a circling motion near his head.

"Mad?" finished the Professor. "Oh, no, no. I'm sure she's not mad."

"But then, what should we think?" asked Susan.

"It's all a matter of logic, my dear," the Professor explained. "There are only three possibilities. One, your sister is telling lies. Two, she is mad. Three, she is telling the truth. You just said that she is an honest girl. I just told you she isn't mad. That leaves only one possibility."

"That she's telling the truth," Susan said, almost whispering.

"But we checked the wardrobe and there was

nothing but coats," said Peter. "If she's telling the truth, we should be able to go to Narnia, too. After all, if something is real, it's real all the time."

The Professor looked at Peter and said, "But what if it isn't?"

Neither Susan nor Peter could answer that question.

Susan asked the Professor, "But what about the time? Lucy said she was gone for many hours in Narnia, but only a few moments had passed here."

"It's possible that a different world has a different time than ours. She could be there for days and only a few minutes would have passed here."

The Professor saw that Peter and Susan both looked confused. Finally, he said something that would make sense to both of them. "Maybe just leave it alone."

And that's how the conversation ended.

A few days went by and the children said no more about Narnia. Lucy felt better because Peter kept Edmund from teasing her. It seemed that they were not going to have any more adventures in Narnia.

Then one day a tour group visited the house. The Professor's house was very famous, and the housekeeper sometimes gave tours, showing guests the Library, the armor and all the pictures. The housekeeper had told the children to stay out of the way of the tours, but on this day, they didn't hear the group until it was very close.

"Quick," said Susan. "We have to hide."

So all four of them ran into the Library. But then it seemed the group was coming from another direction straight toward the Library.

"Into the Wardrobe Room," said Peter.

So they hurried into the extra room with the wardrobe and shut the door. They thought they were safe, but then the doorknob started turning.

"Oh no! Into the Wardrobe," whispered Susan and they all got in, scared and out of breath. Peter was the last in and he pulled the door of the wardrobe closed, but not all the way. He remembered that you should never shut a wardrobe door all the way.

Chapter Six

Into the Forest

Susan was the first to speak. "Isn't it cold in here?"

Peter was next. "And I've got something sticking in my back. Hey, there's something wet by my feet."

Edmund wanted to get out of the wardrobe because he knew what was happening. But Susan said, "Oh! I'm sitting against a tree."

"And over there," added Peter. "More trees. And snow! Say, this looks like Lucy's forest!"

The children walked into the pale light of a winter's day.

"Lu," said Peter seriously. "I'm truly sorry for not believing you."

"Me too," said Susan.

Lucy just smiled and said, "It's all right. Now, let's go find Mr. Tumnus!"

"Of course," agreed Susan. "But first, let's put on these coats so we won't catch a cold."

The coats were adult-sized, so they looked more like king's and queen's robes on the children. But they were warm and soft, and the children were glad to wear them. They started off into Narnia, following Peter since he was the oldest.

After a moment, Edmund said, "Why don't we go more to the left so we can get to the lamppost?"

Everyone turned and stared at him. He had forgotten to pretend that he had never been here.

Peter said angrily, "So you really were here! You made Lucy seem like a liar, but *you* are the liar. You really are such a monster."

The girls gave mean looks to Edmund then walked away.

Edmund said nothing but thought very cruel things about his sisters and Peter.

Soon, Peter asked Lucy to lead since she was the most experienced in Narnia.

"I'd like you to meet Mr. Tumnus," she said and walked quickly through the trees all the way to the Faun's house. Lucy was very excited for everyone to meet the Faun, but what she found there was very upsetting. The door was broken down and snow was getting inside the cave. All the dishes were smashed on the floor, and the picture of Mr. Tumnus's father had been cut with a knife. Peter picked up a piece of paper from the floor.

He read it aloud, "'Mr. Faun Tumnus has been taken prisoner by the Queen of Narnia. The charge is High Treason against the Queen and enjoying the company of humans.

Signed MAUGRIM, Captain of the Secret Police.'"

"Oh no!" Lucy cried. "Mr. Tumnus is in trouble because of me. We have to find him."

"Who is this Queen of Narnia?" Peter asked.

"She's a terrible lady called the White Witch," Lucy answered. "She's the one who has made it always winter in Narnia, and never Christmas."

Peter and Susan discussed what to do. They wanted to help Mr. Tumnus, but they didn't have any food and they didn't know where to go.

Suddenly, Lucy said, "Look, there's a bird.

Maybe I can talk to him. 'Mr. Robin, can you please tell us how to find Mr. Tumnus the Faun?'"

The bird flew to the next tree and looked back. Lucy followed him and called for the others. The four children began following the bird without thinking about it. Every time the bird stopped on a tree branch, it would look back at the children. Soon, the winter sun became stronger and made the area brighter.

Edmund was not happy about where they were going. It didn't look like the way to the Queen's house at all. And he was terribly hungry. He pulled Peter back away from the girls.

"Peter, we don't know if we can trust this bird. We don't even know how to get back to the wardrobe."

Peter, who was still very mad at Edmund, thought he was right in this case.

"Oh, I didn't think of that," he said. "And it does seem like we are lost."

Chapter Seven

A Day with the Beavers

As the boys were talking behind them, the girls stopped suddenly.

"Where did the robin go?" cried Lucy. She couldn't see the bird anywhere.

But then Susan saw something moving behind the trees. Was it an animal? Was it friendly?

She said, "There's something behind that tree to the left."

"Yes, I see it," replied Peter, walking up to Susan.

"What is it?" asked Lucy.

"I don't know, but it doesn't want to be seen," answered Peter.

"We should go home," said Susan.

"But we're lost," Edmund said and they all knew he was right.

At that moment, the creature behind the trees

came out into the sunlight. It was a beaver with dark fur and whiskers. It put its hand up to its mouth to signal the children to be quiet. He then ran a few feet away and turned. This time he made the signal to follow.

Peter asked, "What do you think, Lucy? Should we follow it?"

"I think it looks like a nice beaver, so I say yes."

Edmund wasn't sure what a nice beaver looks like, but Susan and Peter agreed with Lucy. The children didn't know the way home, so they followed him. After a moment, the beaver popped his head out from behind a tree.

"We can't talk here. It's not safe," the beaver said. He explained the trees were able to hear them and might tell the Queen. "We need to go deeper into the forest."

The four children went further to a very dark spot in between four trees. They stood close together and the beaver asked a question.

"Are you the humans I've heard about?"

"Yes, I suppose we are," answered Peter. "And pardon me for being rude, but how do we know you are a friend?"

The beaver said, "Of course, of course." And he held up Lucy's handkerchief that Mr. Tumnus had used. "Now you know you can trust me. Mr. Tumnus asked me to help you if I ever met you. Now that Aslan has come back, we finally have hope."

When the children heard the word Aslan, a very strange thing happened. Sometimes in a dream you hear something you don't understand, but you know it has an important meaning. It could be a scary meaning that turns your dream into a nightmare. Or it could be a wonderful meaning that you remember all your life. The children had this same feeling now. Though they didn't know who or what Aslan was, each of them felt something jump inside. Edmund felt very scared. Peter felt brave. Susan smelled something delicious and heard beautiful music. And Lucy felt like she had just woken up and remembered it was the start of the school holidays.

Lucy was still worried about her friend the Faun, but the beaver invited them to his house where they could talk and have some dinner. They were all hungry, so everyone agreed with the beaver's plan. They followed him for more than an hour through the darkest part of the forest. Suddenly, the beaver stopped and the children, who were really very hungry by that time, looked down into a beautiful valley. The river at the bottom of the valley was frozen and a dam had been built across it.

Susan said politely, "Mr. Beaver, what a lovely dam." All the children then remembered that beavers build dams and that this one must be Mr. Beaver's work.

The beaver shook his head modestly, "Well, it's nothing. It's not really finished."

Out in the middle of the dam was a funny-looking house with a hole in the roof from which smoke was coming. This reminded the children of cooking and they became even hungrier.

Edmund was also hungry, but he noticed something the other children did not. He followed the river with his eyes and saw two hills. He was sure those were the hills the White Witch told him about. "So her house must be close by," he thought. He remembered what she had said about Turkish Delight and becoming a King!

The beaver led the children along the top of the dam toward the funny-looking house. It was icy, and they had to watch their step. The beaver opened the front door and said, "Mrs. Beaver! These are the human boys and girls we have heard about!"

In the middle of the cozy room sat a nice old lady beaver using a sewing machine. She jumped up when she saw the children.

"Finally, you've come! I never thought I'd live to see this day. I have potatoes on the stove and hot water in the kettle. Mr. Beaver, you go and get some fish, please."

Peter went with Mr. Beaver, who caught a lot of fish quite quickly. Meanwhile, the girls helped

Mrs. Beaver set the table and cut the bread and prepare the frying pan for the fish. Lucy noticed the Beavers' home was quite different from the Faun's. There were no books, but there were hams and onions hanging from the ceiling and tools and fishing rods hanging on the walls. When the two fishermen returned and put the cleaned fish in the pan, the children wanted them to cook as soon as possible. Finally, when the fish was done, everyone sat on their stools and Mrs. Beaver poured the drinks. There was milk for the children and beer for Mr. Beaver. They all ate their fill of fish and potatoes. After dinner, Mrs. Beaver brought out a delicious smelling marmalade cake from the oven. She served it with hot tea. When the last dessert plates were cleared from the table, Mr. Beaver lit his pipe and looked out the window.

"Lucky for us that it's snowing again," he said. "That means if anyone followed us, they won't find our footprints in the snow."

Chapter Eight

What Happened After Dinner

"Thank you very much for that yummy dinner," said Lucy politely. "But now, please tell us what happened to Mr. Tumnus."

"Oh, dear. It's bad, very bad," began Mr. Beaver. "He was taken away by the police. Taken all the way to *her* house."

"And who is 'her'?" asked Susan.

"The White Witch, of course, dearie," said Mrs. Beaver, shaking her head. "And she will turn him to stone, like a statue."

"But there must be something we can do for him!" Lucy cried. "It's all because of me." She had tears in her eyes.

"Let's go to her house right now. He saved my sister, so I have to do something," said Peter bravely.

"No, no, my boy," said Mr. Beaver. "*You* can't

do anything, but Aslan—"

There was that name again. The children had that strange feeling again, like hearing good news or seeing the first flowers of spring.

"Who is Aslan?" asked Susan.

"Oh, my word. You don't know, child?" Mr. Beaver asked, surprised. "Aslan is the King of the whole forest. He's been away for a long time. I've never seen him, nor did my father. But now we hear that he's back in Narnia, and he can save Mr. Tumnus, if anyone can."

"But won't the Queen turn Aslan to stone, too?" asked Edmund.

"Of course not! The very idea!" Mr. Beaver seemed upset. "She could only look him in the eye, I'd bet. Maybe not even that. There's a poem we have about the great Aslan...

> *Wrong will change to right*
> *When Aslan comes in sight*
> *When we hear his mighty roar,*
> *Sadness will be no more*
> *When he shows his fearsome teeth,*
> *Winter will go beneath*

And when he shakes his golden head,
All will be Spring instead.

"And you'll meet him soon enough. I'm in charge of leading you to him," finished Mr. Beaver proudly.

"Is, is Aslan a man?" asked Lucy.

"Is Aslan a man? No, no, no. Don't you know who the King of Beasts is? He's a lion, of course. *The* Lion!" Mr. Beaver said loudly.

"We didn't know," began Susan. "So is it, uh, *safe* for us to meet him?"

"He's a lion, so of course it isn't safe!" Mr. Beaver said, almost angrily.

"Anyone who meets him will surely be afraid," said Mrs. Beaver more kindly than her husband. "But he's good, dearie. Just wait until you see him. You'll know what I mean."

"Well, I can't wait to meet him," said Peter.

"And you will very soon, my boy. Tomorrow we shall see him at the Stone Table," said Mr. Beaver.

"But what about Mr. Tumnus?" Lucy was still worried about her friend.

"The best thing you can do for him is to let Aslan help him." Mr. Beaver replied. "Of course, you have a part in helping, too. There's another of our old poems. It goes like this:

> *When human flesh and human bone*
> *Sit upon Narnia's throne*
> *The evil time will be done and gone.*

"You've come to help set things right in Narnia, don't you doubt it," Mrs. Beaver said, smiling at the children. "You're the first humans ever to come to Narnia."

"But what about the Witch? Isn't she human?" asked Peter.

"Ha! She's not one bit human. Her mother was a genie and her father was a giant!" Mr. Beaver said, shaking his head.

"And she's been waiting for four humans like you children. Waiting many years, I hear," added Mrs. Beaver. "If she knew there were exactly four of you, why, you'd be in quite a lot of danger."

"Why exactly four?" asked Peter.

"A legend says that when four humans come

to Narnia, they will become Queens and Kings and sit on the thrones at Cair Paravel, the capital city. And once those four thrones are filled with humans, the White Witch will lose all her power in Narnia."

The room got quiet after these words until Lucy suddenly said, "Hey, where's Edmund?"

Everyone looked around and saw that Edmund was not in the room. They all raced outside calling, "Edmund! Edmund!" But they saw no sign of him, not even footprints.

They went back in the beavers' house and Susan cried out, "This is terrible! Oh, I wish we'd never come."

"Mr. Beaver, what are you doing?" asked Peter when he saw him pulling on his boots. "Are you going to look for Edmund?"

"Certainly not. I'm getting ready to leave here. We must be away at once."

"Yes, let's go," agreed Susan. "We have to find him."

"I'm sorry, my girl," said Mr. Beaver, trying to be gentle. "But I already know where he went, and we cannot go after him. He surely went to the White Witch's house."

The others were so surprised that they couldn't speak for a moment.

"The Witch's house?" Susan finally said. "How do you know?"

"Because I've seen the look in his eyes before. If you live in Narnia for a long time, like I have, you can tell. He's been with the Witch and eaten something she gave him."

The children didn't want to believe it, but deep inside they knew it was probably true. Edmund had been acting especially mean since returning from Narnia and hadn't wanted to follow the bird or the beaver. Maybe he had had his own plan all along.

"Still, he's our brother," said Peter. "We have to look for him, no matter what he's done."

"No, no, no," said Mrs. Beaver. "If you all go there, then the Witch will have what she wants. You will be turned to stone at once. She will want to keep Edmund alive so she can catch you three. Believe me. The best chance for your brother is to meet Aslan tomorrow."

"Now let's think a minute about when Edmund

slipped away. That could be important," said Mr. Beaver. "Did he hear about Aslan?"

"Yes, I think so. He asked if the Queen could turn him into stone," said Susan.

"But did he hear us talking about meeting Aslan at the Stone Table?" asked Mrs. Beaver.

For that question, no one had an answer.

But Mr. Beaver said quickly, "There's one thing I do know. As soon as Edmund tells her where you are, she'll come here. So we need to leave NOW!"

Chapter Nine

In the Witch's House

And now you need to hear what happened to Edmund. Even though the dinner was delicious, Edmund couldn't really enjoy it because he was thinking only of Turkish Delight. Since it was magic food, his memory of it made it seem twice as good as regular food. And he was upset with his sisters and Peter because it seemed they were ignoring him as they talked with Mr. and Mrs. Beaver. That wasn't really true, but Edmund believed it. When he heard about meeting Aslan at the Stone Table, he felt the same terrible feeling as when he first heard about Aslan in the forest. He decided he would go to the Queen's house by himself. So, he started to slip quietly toward the door.

At the same time Mr. Beaver was saying the poem about sitting on Narnia's throne, Edmund was turning the doorknob. And before Mrs. Beaver said the White Witch was not human at all, he was already outside and closing the door quietly.

Please don't think Edmund was a bad brother and that he wanted the Witch to turn his brother and sisters to stone. But he really wanted more Turkish Delight, and he wanted to be a King to get back at Peter for calling him a monster. He didn't let himself think that the Witch would do anything terrible. He thought the Faun and the beavers were just making up stories. They couldn't be true.

"Because she was really nice to me," he thought. "Much nicer than Peter or Susan!" But deep inside himself he knew this wasn't true. He knew the White Witch was a terrible person.

When he was walking across the dam, he realized he'd forgotten his coat. The sun was low in the sky now, and it was getting colder. It was snowing, as Mr. Beaver had said, and Edmund couldn't see very well. There was no road, so he had to walk over trees and through deep snow. He kept falling down and soon he wanted to give up and go back to the beavers' house.

But instead of turning around, Edmund imagined all he would do as King of Narnia. "Build some roads first," he thought. And then he imagined how big his palace would be, with his own cinema and train line. He was just getting a bit happier thinking about this when suddenly the weather got worse. The snow stopped and the wind started to blow. He was freezing cold. But the moon came out and helped him see better. He finally found the end of the big river and saw a smaller one. He followed that river for a while until he saw the two hills. And there between the hills, just as the Witch had said, was a small castle. The castle had many pointed towers that looked scary in the moonlight.

But there was nothing else to do but walk up to the house. He was surprised to see no one guarding the gate. In fact, it was wide open. He walked into a courtyard and stopped suddenly. In the middle of the yard was a huge lion, ready to jump. Edmund was so scared that he couldn't move. He waited and waited, but the lion didn't move. So Edmund took a few steps forward, sure the lion would jump on him. But still the lion didn't move.

Then Edmund remembered what the beavers had said about the Witch turning animals to stone. "So this is a stone lion," he thought. He was still scared, in case he was wrong, but he walked up to the lion's face. He put his hand on it quickly. Stone! He couldn't believe he had been scared of a statue, but it looked so real in the moonlight.

As he walked away from the lion, Edmund thought that this could be the great Aslan the beavers had talked about. "He doesn't look so great now," Edmund thought.

He continued walking across the yard and saw many statues of dwarfs, wolves, bears, foxes and mountain cats. There were even magical creatures like centaurs and dragons. Edmund saw a huge man with a long beard that must have been a giant. After passing the giant, Edmund saw a small light coming from a door and he crossed over to it. In front of the door lay a large wolf. Of course, Edmund thought it was a stone wolf, so he started to step over it.

"Who is it?" asked the wolf in a deep voice. "Stop, tell me who you are."

Edmund almost fell over from surprise. "Please, sir, it is Edmund. I'm the human boy that the Queen met in the forest. I have news for her. My brother and sisters are in Narnia, close to here. I think she wants to see them."

The wolf told Edmund to stay by the door while he delivered the message to the Queen.

While the wolf was gone, Edmund felt very cold and scared. But soon, the wolf came back and invited him inside.

"The Queen will see you now. Lucky for you, or not so lucky," the wolf said with a scary smile.

Edmund walked inside with the wolf and found himself in a long hall full of statues. He went past a statue of a faun and wondered if it was Lucy's friend, Mr. Tumnus. Then he saw the Queen sitting on a large throne.

Before Edmund could say anything, the Queen yelled, "You've come alone!"

"But, your Majesty, I've brought my brother and sisters to Narnia. They are here, with the beavers just down the river." Then Edmund told her about Aslan.

She yelled again, "It can't be true! Are you lying to me?"

"No, no, your Majesty. I heard them talking about Aslan."

"Bring the sleigh," she ordered the dwarf who was standing by her side. "And take off the bells. We don't want to be heard."

Chapter Ten

The Spell Begins to Break

Now we must see what the Beavers and the three children did after they discovered Edmund missing.

When they heard Mr. Beaver yell "NOW!" everyone started putting their coats and shoes on. Everyone except Mrs. Beaver. She ran around the small room gathering ham and bread, tea and matches.

Susan cried, "Mrs. Beaver, what are you doing?"

"Well, of course, I'm making a food bundle for each of us. Do you think we'll go to the Stone Table with nothing to eat? It's a long way, dearie."

Peter was getting worried every minute they waited to leave. "Please hurry, Mrs. Beaver. The White Witch is on her way here right now."

"Yes, yes, I know. Just hand me some of those handkerchiefs and I'll wrap up a bundle for each of us. A small one for little Lucy, of course."

Finally, she was done and Mr. Beaver helped her with her boots. "I guess my sewing machine is too heavy to bring," she said quietly to her husband.

"That's right, my dear. We have to leave it here," he said patiently.

They all went out the door with their food bundles. The moon was shining brightly as they started to walk with Mr. Beaver in the front, followed by Lucy, then Peter, Susan and Mrs. Beaver at the end of the line. Mr. Beaver led them along the lower side of the valley so they would stay hidden.

Lucy thought it was a very pretty scene when they first started. The snow-topped trees shone in the moonlight, the stars were very bright, and everything was very quiet. But soon, her short legs got tired and her bundle, even though it was lighter than everyone else's, got very heavy. She could only keep her eyes open enough to see Mr. Beaver's flat feet making marks in the snow. Just when she thought she couldn't walk another step, Mr. Beaver disappeared into a hole in the side of a hill. Lucy crawled into the hole and the others after her.

Peter was also tired and his voice was weak. "Where are we? What is this place?"

Mr. Beaver replied, "It's an old hiding place for beavers. We need some sleep and we will be safe here."

Lucy and the others sat down quite close to each other since the hole was very small. Mrs. Beaver handed around a bottle with something quite strong and warm to drink. After that, they all lay down and went to sleep immediately.

The next moment (or so it seemed to Lucy, though it had really been several hours), Lucy sat up wide awake. The others were also sitting up with wide eyes and open mouths. They heard a sound that made them very afraid: the jingling of bells.

Mr. Beaver raced out of the hole while the others sat in the dark, cold hole. After a few minutes of fearful waiting, they heard voices. But they weren't angry or mean voices. They sounded happy.

Suddenly, Mr. Beaver stuck his head into the hole with a smile on his face. "It's ok, everyone. You can come out!"

The three children and Mrs. Beaver came out of the hole looking sleepy, with dirt and leaves all over their clothes and hair.

"Over here," Mr. Beaver shouted from the top of a small hill. "You won't believe it. You know Narnia has had a long winter but never Christmas. Well, look at this."

Mr. Beaver was pointing to something that seemed to the children to be impossible. It was a sleigh pulled by brown reindeer with bells. In the driver's seat was a person who would be known to children in all parts of the world, not only in Narnia. He was a very big man with a long white beard and he wore a red robe with a hood. The children were so surprised, they became very still. It couldn't be Father Christmas, could it?

The man spoke. "It's been a long time, but I've come now. Aslan is moving closer and the Witch's magic is getting weaker."

The children couldn't say anything, but they felt a joy inside that was hard to describe.

"I've got presents for each of you," Father Christmas said. "Mrs. Beaver, this is a better sewing machine than the one you have. I'll take it by your house when I go."

"Oh, thank you, sir. I appreciate it very much," Mrs. Beaver said, doing a small curtsey.

"And Mr. Beaver, your dam will be repaired with a new gate by the time you return."

Mr. Beaver looked so pleased that he couldn't think of anything to say.

"As for the human boy, Peter," Father Christmas continued. "I have a shield and sword. These are not toys but tools, and you will need them soon enough. Use them well."

Peter took the weapons with a serious look and bowed in thanks.

"For Susan, there are bow and arrows. I do not want you to fight in the battle that is coming. Use these only if you need them. And this horn, when you blow it, will bring help to you wherever you are."

"And, finally, for Lucy, here is a bottle of liquid that will heal any hurt. It only takes a few drops. And there is also a small knife to protect yourself."

Lucy took the two presents and said, "I don't know that I will be brave enough to fight."

"I understand, dear girl. Of course, I do not

want you in the battle. It is terrible when women have to fight."

Father Christmas wanted to change the subject, so he said with a happier look, "And here's something for everyone."

Suddenly, Father Christmas was holding a large tray with five teacups and saucers, a bowl of sugar, a bottle of cream and a large teapot full of hot tea.

He handed the tray to Mr. Beaver and Peter. Then he yelled, "Merry Christmas! Long live Aslan!" as the sleigh pulled out of sight.

Mr. Beaver and Peter carried the tray down to the cave. The group ate the ham and bread from their bundles with the delicious tea. Soon, though, Mr. Beaver said they'd better get going.

Chapter Eleven

Aslan is Nearer

While the three children and the Beavers were celebrating Christmas, Edmund was having a much worse time. He was waiting for the Witch to start being nice to him, like she was the first time they met. But she didn't speak to him at all.

Finally, he bravely said, "Excuse me, your Majesty. You said when I came to your house, I could have some Turkish Delight."

She looked very meanly at him but ordered one of the dwarfs to bring him some food. When the dwarf came, he brought only a hard piece of bread and a small cup of water.

Edmund tried the bread, but it was so hard that he could not chew it well.

"I don't want this," he said sadly, but the Witch looked at him with such a terrible expression on her face that he started eating it again.

The dwarf brought the sleigh to the courtyard, and Edmund got in it next to the Witch. She called for the big wolf named Maugrim, whom Edmund had thought was a stone animal. She told him to take one of his fellow wolves and run to the Beavers house. She told them to kill whoever was there.

Then she said, "I will meet you at the Stone Table. If you see the human children before I get there, you know what to do."

The wolves went quickly down the valley to the beavers' house, but, of course, it was empty. Fortunately, the animals could not follow the tracks of the children and the Beavers because the snow had covered them up.

While the wolves were on their mission, the dwarf, the Witch and Edmund rode in the snow through the forest. Edmund was terribly cold since he had no coat and the Witch did not offer to share hers. The snow piled on his front until he was wet all the way through. Even worse than the cold was Edmund's feeling of disappointment about not having any more Turkish Delight and not being made a King.

The Witch had said so many things to make him believe she was a good person, but those were all lies. He was surprised how silly her words sounded to him now. He wanted to be with his sisters and brother very badly. Yes, even Peter. He just closed his eyes and told himself it was a bad dream that would all be over soon.

The sleigh moved on through the night and into the next morning. The snow had stopped and it was getting lighter as the sun came up.

Suddenly, the Witch shouted, "Stop! What is this?"

She pointed to a group of animals around a table, looking like they were having a party. A squirrel family with two children, two satyrs, a dwarf and an old fox were eating and drinking and laughing. Edmund smelled the delicious food and remembered his hard bread the night before. He also saw holly decorations and a plum pudding. Oh, he was very hungry!

The whole party stopped suddenly when they saw the sleigh and the White Witch. The squirrel children made terrified sounds.

"What is this?" the Witch repeated. "Where

did you get all this? If you don't speak, I will beat you with this whip," she said, pointing to the whip that the dwarf used on the reindeer.

"Your Majesty," said the fox finally, "we were given this food and drink by Father Christmas. And may I drink a toast to your good health."

When the Witch heard the name 'Father Christmas,' she jumped from the sleigh and ran toward the party.

"It can't be!" she yelled. "He's not been here. You are lying, all of you!"

"But he has. He's been here. I tell you, he has," said the squirrel bravely.

The White Witch became so angry, she pulled out her wand and waved it toward the group around the table.

Edmund yelled, "Please, no. Don't!" but it was too late. All the creatures were turned to stone in an instant, just as they were. The father squirrel had a fork in its mouth and it stuck there. Even the plum pudding turned into stone.

As she got back into the sleigh, the Witch slapped Edmund hard across the face.

"Do not ask for forgiveness for those who

have betrayed their Queen," she said.

Edmund's face hurt from the slap, but nothing was more painful than seeing the small stone animals as the sleigh pulled away. They would sit there day and night for many years until they fell apart. What a pity!

A little while after they started again, Edmund noticed the sleigh was slowing down. The snow was melting and water splashed against the reindeer's legs. Edmund saw it was becoming foggy and felt it was warmer than before. The dwarf tried and tried to make the reindeer go faster, but they couldn't pull the sleigh over the rocks and dirt, which were appearing as the snow melted faster and faster. Finally, the sleigh stopped again and Edmund heard a familiar sound all around. Water! Running, rushing, splashing water everywhere. The streams and rivers that had been completely frozen were turning into water again. Snow was falling from the trees as it melted and green grass was showing all over the land.

Edmund felt something inside jump, though he didn't know why. Maybe there was hope after all. The dream was coming to an end.

The Witch was angry, but she said, "We walk from here."

She told the dwarf to tie Edmund's hands behind his back and to hold the end of the rope so he couldn't escape. In this way, the three walked on the dirt path that had been covered with snow just a few minutes before. The dwarf was very mean to Edmund and every time he slipped in the mud, the dwarf hit him with the whip. Edmund didn't like being beaten, of course, but he kept his mind on what was happening all around him. There were white and yellow flowers coming up on both sides of the path. Edmund heard a bird

sing, followed by many birds singing together. The Witch didn't seem to notice all the birds flying around and singing. She just yelled at Edmund and the dwarf to move faster. The trees were also growing their leaves back so that the forest was turning a light green color.

Finally, the dwarf said, "This is not a small melting. It's *spring*! The winter is gone. It must be Aslan coming that's doing this."

The Witch yelled at the dwarf, "Say that name again and you will DIE!"

Chapter Twelve

Peter's First Battle

In a far distant part of the forest, the Beavers and the three children were walking through what seemed to them a wonderful dream. It was so warm that they took off their coats. They were delighted with each new flower, each delicious smell, each bird song. All around them, winter had turned to spring in just a few hours. They weren't sure, as the Witch was, that this sudden melting meant that Aslan had come to Narnia. All they understood was that the Witch's power was fading and that she would no longer be able to use her sleigh to get to the Stone Table. This gave the group more time to enjoy the beautiful scene all around them.

It was just about evening when Mr. Beaver said, "Almost there."

They followed him up a hill with soft moss

growing on the ground and tall trees spaced quite far apart. Lucy and the others were tired, but not so tired that they wanted to fall down. Just the kind of pleasant tiredness that you get near the end of a long day outside. When they came to the top of the hill, they saw an amazing sight.

There were green fields and forests wherever they looked, except for one spot to the East. In that spot, a moving sparkling blue-green color caught their eye.

"I don't believe it! It's the sea!" exclaimed Peter.

In one of the fields close to them, they saw a large tent made of yellow silk with red ropes and a banner with a lion. To the west of the tent, they saw what must be the Stone Table on top of a slope. It looked very old and had strange markings on the side. Suddenly, they heard music coming from the direction of the tent. It was the kind of music that announced something special had arrived. The children and the beavers walked down the hill and stood near the tent. They were all in awe. There were centaurs, unicorns, pelicans, eagles and a very large dog. Standing in the middle of a circle of these animals and magical creatures was Aslan himself.

It's hard to describe what the group felt when they saw Aslan at last. It seemed he was wonderful and terrible at the same time. Some people don't believe this is possible, but the

children now understood that it is very possible. Aslan's face held large serious eyes that were too hard to look at for very long.

None of them could move and finally Mr. Beaver said, "Go on. Human children meet him first."

Susan said to Peter, "You're the oldest. Go on."

Peter pulled out his sword to salute the King of the Beasts and said, "We are here, Aslan."

Aslan spoke then in a kind, deep voice.

"Welcome, Peter, Susan and Lucy. And welcome He-Beaver and She-Beaver."

They all felt more comfortable after he welcomed them.

"But there were four children, were there not? Where is the fourth?" Aslan asked.

Mr. Beaver answered before the children could explain. "He has gone to the White Witch. He has betrayed us."

Peter wanted to defend Edmund since he was his brother.

"It was partly my fault. He knew I was angry with him and he went to the wrong side."

"But we need to save him, Aslan. Please!" Lucy begged.

"It will be harder than you think, but it will be done," Aslan promised. In that moment, Lucy thought she saw some sadness in Aslan's eyes. But then he shouted, "Let us prepare the grand meal!" He then asked some of the female creatures to help Lucy and Susan get washed and dressed for the celebration.

The girls went off to one side of the large tent and Peter stood with Aslan. "Let me show you where you will be King," said Aslan. They walked to the eastern side of the field where they could see the sea. Close to the sea, shining in the setting sun, was a castle with many windows.

"That castle is called Cair Paravel," explained Aslan. "It has four thrones, one for each of you children. You will be High King since you are the oldest."

Peter was about to say something, but a strange sound was heard at that moment. It was the horn that Father Christmas had given Susan. Peter was unsure what it meant at first, but then he saw the animals and creatures running around. Susan was in danger!

He ran as fast as he could in the direction of the tent. Lucy was running toward him looking very scared. Then he saw why. A huge gray wolf was chasing Susan! She was trying to climb a tree to escape it, but she couldn't pull herself up to a higher branch. The wolf was just about to bite her leg. Peter charged toward the wolf, though he felt very scared inside. He swung his sword but missed the wolf. The wolf turned toward Peter angrily. It jumped up on its back legs and Peter moved under it. He stuck his sword deep into the wolf's heart. The wolf fell on top of Peter and,

for a moment, Peter wasn't sure if it was dead or alive. Then Peter pushed the wolf off and saw that it was dead. He pulled his sword out and stood looking at it. Susan came down from the tree, and they held each other while shaking and crying.

Aslan saw another wolf hiding in the trees. He yelled to the animals and magical creatures to follow it.

"He will lead you to the White Witch. Then you can take back the fourth child," he ordered.

Aslan then walked over to Peter.

"Well done, Peter. Now don't forget to clean your sword."

Peter wiped his sword on the grass and Aslan said, "We will now call you Sir Peter the Wolfkiller. Be brave, be honest and always remember to clean your sword."

Chapter Thirteen

Deep Magic
from the Beginning of Time

Let us now go back to see what was happening
with Edmund. He, the White Witch and the dwarf
had walked and walked. Edmund thought they
had walked farther than anyone could ever walk.
He was so tired that he didn't notice how hungry
and thirsty he was. Finally, they stopped under
some trees and Edmund fell down flat on his
face and didn't move. He really didn't care what
happened to him if he could just stop moving.

The Witch and the dwarf were talking in
whispers near him.

"We can't reach them now. They are already
at the Stone Table," said the dwarf, meaning the
other children had met Aslan.

"I hope the wolves have done their job and
bring me good news," said the Witch. Then she
had a different thought.

"I wonder what would happen if only three of the thrones in Cair Paravel were filled. Would that change the legend that says when four humans come to Narnia, I will lose my powers?"

The dwarf was not sure anything could change the legend now that Aslan was close, but he didn't dare say that to the Queen.

"What should we do with him"—the dwarf pointed to Edmund—"kill him now or save him for bargaining?"

"I cannot risk having him rescued. Let us get rid of him at once!"

So the Queen decided to kill Edmund and the dwarf began to prepare his knife to do the job.

At that moment, a wolf came running and stopped in front of the Witch. He was almost out of breath, but he spoke quickly.

"They are at the Stone Table with *Him*. Maugrim is dead, killed by one of the human children. I saw it all from behind some bushes. We must run away quickly!"

"Ugh! I will not run away," yelled the Witch. "But I will get rid of these humans, starting with him!"

She then pulled Edmund up from the ground and tied him to a tree. The dwarf pulled Edmund's shirt back so that his neck was showing. The dwarf was just about to use the knife on Edmund's throat when there were shouts coming from all around. Edmund could hear horses running and wings flapping. The Witch screamed and then Edmund was being untied. Someone with big, strong arms was holding him. The voices around him said, "It's ok, child. Here's some wine. You're all right."

These same voices then started arguing. "Where's the Witch?" "I thought you had her." "I didn't see her." "I was chasing the dwarf." "Well, I can't do everything myself." It was all too much for Edmund and he fainted.

Soon all of the creatures who had rescued Edmund, all the unicorns and deer and birds, started walking back toward the Stone Table. A large unicorn carried Edmund on its back. None of the creatures noticed a strange sight near the tree where Edmund was almost killed.

It was dark by then, but the forest was brightly lit by the moon. There was a tree and a large rock shining in the moonlight. If you were nearby, you might think the large rock was really a small man in a ball shape on the ground. You would also see the tree walk toward the large rock and start talking. These kinds of things happen in Narnia. The tree was really the Witch and the large rock was really the dwarf. The Witch had used her magic to hide from the creatures who rescued Edmund.

Back at the tent, the other children slept on comfortable cushions after their long, exciting day. In the morning, Mrs. Beaver brought the good news of Edmund's rescue. She said that Edmund was now talking with Aslan and the children could see him after breakfast. They ate quickly and when they came out of the tent, they saw Edmund and Aslan in deep conversation. No one heard what they were saying, but Edmund never forgot Aslan's words as long as he lived.

Soon Aslan led Edmund over to the other children.

"Here is Edmund. You do not need to talk about what happened."

Edmund looked at his brother and sisters

and said, "I'm sorry." He reached out his hand to shake theirs, but Susan and Lucy ran to give him a hug. Peter patted Edmund on the back and said, "That's all right." The children wanted to say more to each other, but they didn't know how to begin.

Just then, a leopard came up to Aslan with the Witch's dwarf.

"This dwarf would like to speak with you, Sire," the leopard said.

Aslan looked at the dwarf and asked, "What do you have to say?"

"The Queen of Narnia would like to talk with you," began the dwarf. "She asks for her safety to be assured when she comes here."

"Tell her that she may come here if she leaves her wand at that tree over there." Aslan pointed with his huge paw to an oak tree to the side of the tent.

Soon, the White Witch came from the top of the hill and walked straight over to Aslan. They stood together for a moment, though the Witch did not look into Aslan's eyes. The children who had not met the Witch felt cold go through them, even though it was bright and sunny outside.

"There is a traitor here, Aslan," the Witch began, and everyone knew she was talking about Edmund. Edmund might have felt bad about those words before, but after talking with Aslan, he didn't mind them.

"You remember the Deep Magic, don't you?" the Witch continued. "If you've forgotten, I will remind you. The magic law from the very beginning of Narnia says that all traitors are mine to kill if I choose."

"We will fight you if you try to hurt these children," the leopard near Aslan said.

"Don't be stupid. This is a deep magic law that cannot be undone by fighting. If I do not get what is mine by law, all of Narnia will be destroyed by fire and water."

"She is right," said Aslan seriously. "I cannot change it."

Edmund was looking at Aslan the whole time and felt like he was choking. But he kept silent and then he heard Aslan say, "I will talk to the Witch alone."

So everyone went back to the tent while the

Witch and Aslan talked.

Lucy couldn't stand it and she started crying.

"Oh, Edmund," she said, putting her arms around him.

After a very long time, Aslan came back to the tent.

"It is all right," he announced. "The Witch will not harm your brother."

A large sound of relief came over the whole group, as if every person and animal and creature had been holding their breath and finally could breathe again.

Lucy noticed that as the Witch walked away with the dwarf, she looked very happy, which was strange since she had not gotten what she wanted.

Chapter Fourteen

The Witch's Triumph

Everyone wanted to ask Aslan how he had made the Witch change her mind, but he looked so serious that no one spoke to him. Aslan told them to move the camp to another place to the northeast. The children helped the animals and magical creatures pack all the things in the tent and they started walking. They didn't need to hurry, so they enjoyed the sunshine.

Aslan spoke to Peter while they walked. There would be a big battle, he said, starting some time soon.

"The Witch will prepare for the fight near her house and you might be able to catch her there. If you don't win against her at her house, you can fight her and her supporters in the forest. I advise putting the Centaurs in the front because they are the best fighters."

Peter listened but began to wonder why Aslan was telling him all this.

"You will be there, too, won't you?" Peter asked.

"I'm not sure of that," was the only thing Aslan said in reply. Peter noticed Aslan didn't say much after that and looked sad.

When they came to a river, Aslan ordered everyone to make a camp there. Peter asked if it would be better to cross the river and camp on the other side, in case the Witch tried to attack in the night.

"She will not attack us tonight," Aslan said in a tired voice. "But you are thinking like a soldier and that is good."

During their evening meal, all the animals and magical creatures were affected by Aslan's sad mood. The news that he might not be leading the battle was surprising to them.

Lucy and Susan talked about it that night when they were trying to go to sleep.

"I have a feeling something terrible is going to happen," started Susan.

"So do I," replied Lucy.

"It's something about Aslan. I don't know what's bothering him," Susan said in a worried voice.

"Do you think he would leave before the battle begins?" Lucy wondered. "Let's go find him, Susan."

So the two girls left the tent quietly and looked around by the river.

"Over there," Susan whispered, pointing to Aslan walking away from them. They followed him secretly into the forest.

"He's going toward the Stone Table," Lucy said quietly.

The girls noticed that Aslan looked very different now. His tail was dragging the ground and his head hung very low. It seemed like he was very tired. Suddenly, he stopped and turned around.

"Oh, girls," he said seriously. "Why are you following me?"

They tried to explain, but he already knew what they were thinking.

"Please let us come with you, wherever you are going," Lucy begged.

"All right," said Aslan kindly. "But you have to promise to stop and let me go alone when I say it's time."

The girls wondered what 'It's time' meant, but they promised to do as he said.

Lucy walked on Aslan's right side and Susan walked on his left, and he seemed happier to have them with him. Even so, he walked so slowly. Then, he almost fell down.

Susan cried, "Aslan, are you sick?"

"What is wrong? Please tell us," Lucy added.

"No, no. I am not sick. I'm just tired and sad. But if you put your hands on my fur, I will feel better." And so each girl lay a hand near his head and they continued walking like that.

When they got halfway up the slope where the Stone Table was, Aslan stopped. There was a tree with bushes around it.

"And now you must stay here," he said quietly. "You must not move no matter what happens. Good-bye."

This made both girls upset, though they weren't sure why. They kissed Aslan and patted his hair. Finally, he walked away from them with sad eyes.

As Lucy and Susan sat down in the bushes, they looked up to the top of the slope and saw many magical creatures around the Stone Table. The creatures looked evil and many carried sticks with red fire. Some had terrible teeth and others were so scary that I cannot tell you about them. If I did, the adults would not let you read this book. All of these creatures were on the Witch's side and looked at her with awe.

The Witch was standing next to the Stone Table. When she saw Aslan walking up the hill, she cried "Here he is, the fool! Tie him up!"

Some of the dwarfs and evil apes went toward Aslan with ropes. Susan and Lucy waited for Aslan to fight them off. But he didn't do anything and let them roll him over and tie his four legs together. Then they began to pull Aslan up the rest of the hill by his legs.

"Wait," the Witch yelled. "First, shave his golden fur."

The evil creatures thought this was very funny and they came toward Aslan with scissors and knives. As his hair fell in long curls to the ground, he began to look smaller and smaller.

"I can't believe we were afraid of him. He's just a big cat," said one of the creatures.

Others teased Aslan by saying, "Here, kitty, kitty. Here's a nice cup of milk. Do you want some mice?"

Lucy was very upset by what she saw and heard. She started crying and Susan held her close.

"To me, he looks more brave and beautiful than ever," Susan said with tears in her eyes.

Now the Witch ordered Aslan's mouth to be tied up and he again allowed the creatures to do this. Now all the creatures saw that he would not harm them, and they started pushing him and spitting on him and kicking him. It was a horrible sight for the girls to see. But they kept their promise to Aslan and did not come out from their hiding place.

Finally, the Witch said it was time for Aslan to be laid on the Stone Table. It took many of the Witch's followers to lift Aslan onto the Table and to tie him to it. Each corner of the Table was lit with a fire stick held by four junior witches. In this firelight, the girls saw the Witch pull out a strange-looking knife. She walked up to Aslan's head. He didn't look at her but at the sky, and his face was sad. The Witch leaned over Aslan and whispered into his ear.

"You think you have saved the human boy by giving your life. Yes, you have saved Narnia as the Deep Magic law says, but you have not saved the boy. I will kill him after you are gone. Think on this as you die hopelessly."

The girls could not watch the Witch take Aslan's life. They covered their eyes and continued crying.

Chapter Fifteen

Deeper Magic from Before the Beginning of Time

The girls sat there for a long time. Finally, the Witch yelled to all her followers.

"We will now fight those human children and all who were on this cat's side." She pointed to Aslan with a mean face. "He cannot hurt us now that he is dead."

All on the Witch's side rushed off quickly. Susan and Lucy watched creatures flying above them and animals run past them, yelling and blowing into pipes. They made a lot of noise, but the girls hardly noticed because they were so sad about what happened to Aslan.

Finally, when the Witch and her group had all left, the girls stood up and walked up to the Stone Table.

It was still night, but the moon gave enough light to see the body of the lion lying on the

Stone Table. They started crying again when they saw it, a cold, dead shell of the great beast who was the King of Narnia. They touched what fur was left near his head and kissed his face. They thought they had cried all their tears, but they cried some more.

At last, Lucy said, "Let's untie his mouth." And when they did, they wiped all the blood away and made his face clean again. It was terrible work, but they felt better when they looked at him.

Then Susan suggested they untie all the ropes around his legs. But the Witch's creatures had pulled the ropes so tight that the girls could not untie them. This made Susan and Lucy even more sad. There aren't words to describe the

girls' sadness as they sat for hours on the Stone Table with Aslan's body.

Lucy finally saw a bit of the sun's light coming from the east. Then she saw some small movement around the large Stone Table. As the morning light poured over the top of the hill, she could see mice all over the table.

"Oh," cried Susan, seeing the mice also. "Go away, you terrible things. Leave him alone."

But Lucy told Susan to look more closely. The mice were not trying to eat Aslan's body. They were chewing the ropes to untie him. Susan and Lucy saw hundreds of small mice tearing at the ropes with their teeth. Finally, the girls pulled the ropes away from Aslan's legs. They thought he looked better now that he wasn't tied up.

The girls walked around the area to warm themselves up. They heard birds singing. They looked off to the east and saw the gray waters of the ocean. The sky was turning reddish-orange. Suddenly, they heard a cracking sound behind them. It sounded like a giant breaking a large plate. They turned back toward the Stone Table and saw that it was split into two pieces. *And*

Aslan was gone!

Lucy cried loudly, "They couldn't even leave his body alone!" She thought the Witch's creatures had come back to take the body away.

But then a voice from behind them said, "No, I am here."

The girls turned around and saw Aslan standing there, looking even bigger and more beautiful than before. His hair had grown back and he was shaking his head.

Susan and Lucy ran to him and spoke at the same time.

"Oh, Aslan! You're not dead!"

"No, not anymore," he said. He put a paw out so the girls could feel that he was real and not a ghost.

"But how?" asked Lucy after she had felt his very real, warm paw.

"The Queen spoke of deep magic from the beginning of time and she was right. But she did not know about even deeper magic that goes back to before the beginning of time. That magic law says that if someone who had done no wrong gives his or her life instead of the traitor, then the death will be undone. The magic can make death work backward."

The girls were still confused, but they were so happy to see Aslan alive that it didn't matter.

Lucy clapped her hands with joy and Aslan jumped up in response. He and the girls ran around the Stone Table and through the trees, laughing and playing as if nothing terrible had happened. They rolled together through some soft grass and lay for a moment, smiling.

Then Aslan jumped up and said, "I feel like roaring now. You'd better put your fingers in your ears."

So the girls pushed their ears closed with their fingers, and Aslan let out the loudest roar that was ever heard in Narnia or anywhere else.

After that, Aslan got serious and said, "We must be off. Jump on my back and we shall run to the Queen's house."

And so the girls climbed up onto Aslan's back and held onto his fur. He started running so fast that it was like being on the fastest racehorse in the world. But it was a smooth ride on soft fur and the girls did not feel scared at all. In fact, it was their favorite part of all in Narnia. They rode past waterfalls and trees and flowers and rocks and caves. All this time, Aslan never made a false step or wondered which way to go. He went straight for the Witch's house, which looked to Lucy and Susan like a toy castle from far away. But when they got closer, they saw it was a real house.

Suddenly, Aslan called to the girls. "Hold tight!" And he jumped over the gate of the castle. Lucy and Susan then saw they were in a large courtyard filled with statues.

Chapter Sixteen

What Happened About the Statues

Aslan went to work at once. He walked up to the lion and breathed on it. Then he did the same to the dwarf near the lion and next the rabbit. Then to some centaurs. All over the courtyard, Aslan breathed on the statues, but at first, nothing seemed to happen. They still didn't move. Then, very slowly, some light appeared behind the stone. The light grew and grew until the gray stone was gone and only the animal or creature could be seen. In this way, all the statues were returned to life.

The courtyard had turned into a zoo with all kinds of animals running around. They ran to Aslan and danced around him. Foxes and dogs and satyrs, dwarfs and tree-women. They made happy noises that grew so loud, Susan and Lucy put their hands over their ears.

When Aslan breathed on the giant, Susan was a bit worried. Would they be safe? But when the giant came alive, he said in a dull voice, "Oh, I must have fallen asleep. But where's that terrible Witch? I'm going to find her and..." Soon some of the birds flew near the giant's ears and explained what had happened. So the giant bowed to Aslan in thanks.

Aslan next went inside the house to free the statues there. When Lucy saw the statue of Mr. Tumnus, she called for Aslan's help. In a few minutes, she was hugging the Faun, and he was crying and dancing at the same time.

After all the statues throughout the house had been freed, everyone gathered back in the courtyard. They wanted to leave the Witch's house, but they found the gate locked. Aslan asked for the giant's help.

"Could you make an exit for us, Mr. Giant?"

"It would be my extreme pleasure, Sire."

And the giant swung his giant club, knocking down some of the wall next to the gate. With another few swings, there was a big hole where the wall used to be. Everyone cheered.

"I beg your pardon," said the giant to the girls. "But do one of you ladies have a handkerchief I could borrow?" He had gotten a bit sweaty with all his hard work.

"I do," Lucy yelled so the giant could hear her. She raised her hand with the handkerchief in it, but the giant picked her off the ground and raised her to his face.

"Oh, sorry, miss," said the giant. "I thought *you* were the handkerchief."

Lucy laughed and tried to wipe the giant's face. Her handkerchief was so small, though, that it was like wiping a mountain with a bit of cloth. He thanked her and put her down on the ground very gently.

"Thank you for trying, miss," the giant said politely.

Aslan then called for silence. "We must go to the battle now. The Witch still has some power and many followers."

The other lion, the first statue that Aslan had freed, began organizing the group. The smaller animals rode on the larger ones. He asked the animals with good noses to lead the group so they could find the Witch quickly. There was a lot of noise and running around as they were preparing.

Lucy and Susan got on Aslan's back. Finally, everyone was ready and the dogs put their noses to the ground. Soon, one of them picked up a scent and the whole group followed.

They hadn't been riding for long when Lucy heard the sound of metal hitting metal. She saw through the trees a large field where a great battle was happening. Lucy saw all the terrible creatures from the night before at the Stone Table. Peter and Edmund had fewer supporters than the Witch. Peter and the Witch herself were fighting in the center of the field. She was holding the knife she had used on Aslan.

When Aslan saw the Witch, he let Lucy and Susan down quickly. Then he roared a most frightening roar and ran toward her. She was very surprised to see him, of course, and she lifted her knife. They rolled on the ground together, and the Witch did not get up again. All the animals and magical creatures that had been freed from the Witch's house ran toward her supporters and started fighting.

Chapter Seventeen

The Hunting of the White Deer

After the Witch's followers saw that she was dead, they ran away into the forest and the fighting was over. Peter and Aslan shook hands, and Lucy noticed how much older and more serious Peter looked. He must have grown a few years in just a few hours during the battle.

Peter told Aslan, "Edmund was the real hero of this battle. He ran straight for the Queen, but instead of trying to hurt her, he went for her wand. He used his sword to knock it out of her hand. That way, she couldn't turn any more of our fighters into stone. But he got hurt very badly."

The children and Aslan ran to where Mrs. Beaver was trying to help Edmund. He had blood all over him and his face was a pale green color. Lucy pulled the bottle Father Christmas had given her out of her pocket.

She poured a few drops of the liquid into Edmund's mouth. She wanted to wait to see if it had worked, but Aslan said there were others who needed help.

She hurried to the other animals and creatures who were badly hurt, pouring drops into their mouths. Aslan went around the field, breathing on those who had been turned to stone. It took some time to help everyone, and then Lucy could go back to see how Edmund was doing.

She was so happy to see that Edmund looked better than she remembered even before they came to Narnia. His face had more color and his eyes were brighter. He looked at Lucy straight in the eyes and said, "Thank you, Lu, for saving me."

Aslan told Edmund that he was to become a knight as a reward for his bravery against the Witch. As Aslan talked with Edmund, Lucy asked Susan if she thought Edmund knew what Aslan had done. How he gave his life so that the Witch wouldn't kill Edmund.

"No, I'm sure he doesn't," whispered Susan.

"And we won't tell him, either. He would feel very bad if he knew."

So Lucy promised to keep quiet about what she and Susan saw at the Stone Table that night.

Aslan used his magic to make a delicious dinner appear right next to the battlefield. They all ate and drank until they were too sleepy to move. The next morning they started walking toward the castle at Cair Paravel, the capital of Narnia. It took them the whole day and part of the next, and they were very tired when they arrived. They had walked all the way to the ocean they had seen on the day they first met Aslan. The children took their socks and shoes off and played on the beach.

However, the next day, they had to act like adults because on that day, they became kings and queens. They put on fine dresses and suits and walked into the main hall, which was decorated with peacock's feathers and gold. Trumpets were sounded and each of the children was crowned by Aslan. All around them the animals and magical creatures yelled, "Long live King Peter!" "Long live Queen Susan!" "Long live King Edmund!"

"Long live Queen Lucy!"

Aslan looked proudly at them as he said, "Human boys and human girls, wear these crowns forever and well!"

Their friends gathered around the thrones when the children sat on them. The new Kings and Queens gave rewards to all the animals that had helped them, Mr. Tumnus, the Beavers and others. They praised all the good centaurs and good dwarfs and the other lion. Then they ate a wonderful meal and danced to beautiful music. From outside they could hear the music of the sea people, who also celebrated the new Kings and Queens of Narnia.

The children noticed about halfway through the party that Aslan was not there. They were worried and spoke to Mr. Beaver about it.

He told them, "It's ok. Aslan has other matters to take care of. He's the King of all the lands around, not only Narnia. He will come and go, so don't worry. He is a *wild* lion after all."

The new Kings and Queens took care of what was left of the Witch's followers. They sent animals to fight them until they heard no more about evil creatures in the forests of Narnia. They also made fair laws and helped the trees from being cut down. When a band of angry giants tried to take over part of Narnia, they fought them back. They also visited lands outside of Narnia and hosted visits from leaders of these lands.

Of course, the children grew up during these years. Peter became a tall man with a broad chest. Susan also grew tall and her hair grew very long. Many men from other lands wanted to marry her. Edmund also became a man, though more serious than Peter. Lucy grew up too but did not change her hair or her high spirits. She was always happy and she was popular among her people.

One year, Mr. Tumnus came to the castle with news that the White Deer had been seen. This was the deer that sometimes visited Narnia. He could make your wish come true if you could catch him. So the Kings and Queens went to find the deer. They saw him entering a thick part of the forest where the horses could not go. King Peter, Queen Susan, King Edmund, and Queen Lucy decided to follow the deer on foot.

As they walked in the direction they had seen the deer go, Susan saw a strange iron tree. "What is this?" she asked.

Edmund looked at it closely and said, "It seems to have a light on the top."

Then King Peter said, "What a silly place for a light. The trees around here are so big that no one can be helped by this light."

The Kings and Queens stared at the strange post for a long time.

Finally, King Edmund said, "This post makes me feel like I've been here before. As if, in a dream."

The rest agreed with him and Queen Lucy added, "I believe if we walk on from this post, we may have some more grand adventures or a big change in our lives."

The others nodded their heads because they felt the same.

Queen Susan then said, "So let us walk from the post and not fear what comes."

They began to walk past the post. In just a moment, they all remembered the name of the iron light. It was a lamppost. And in a moment after that, they were not walking through trees but through fur coats. And in the next moment, they were falling out of the front of the wardrobe. They were not wearing their kings' and queens' clothes and they were not adults. Outside in the hall, they could hear the visitors on the tour led by the housekeeper. No time at all had passed since they had entered the wardrobe!

It seems that the story of the children's adventures has come to an end. But there is one more part of the story. The children wanted to explain to the Professor why four coats in the wardrobe were missing. So they went to his office and told him all that had happened in their years in Narnia. The Professor was an incredible person because he believed everything they said. They wanted to know if they should try to get the coats back, but the Professor just shook his head.

"I don't think you can go back through the wardrobe to Narnia. Someday, though, you'll find your way back there in a different way. And it's best not to talk about this with people, unless you meet someone who has also been to Narnia. You'll know them by how they look."

So now we've come to the real end of the adventures in the wardrobe. But as for the adventures in Narnia, we've only just begun.

Word List

A

□ **about to** 《be –》まさに〜しよう
としている、〜するところだ

□ **across** 熟 slap someone across
the face（人）の顔を平手打ちする
walk across 〜を歩いて渡る

□ **act** 動 ①行動する ②機能する ③演
じる act like an adult 大人のよう
に行動する

□ **add** 動 ①加える、足す ②足し算を
する ③言い添える

□ **adult** 名 大人、成人 act like an
adult 大人のように行動する

□ **adult-sized** 形 大人用の、アダル
トサイズの

□ **adventure** 名 冒険

□ **advise** 動 忠告する、勧める、〔人に〕
アドバイスする

□ **affect** 動 影響を与える

□ **afraid of** 《be –》〜を恐れる、〜を
怖がる

□ **after** 熟 after all やはり、結局
after that その後 go after 〜の後を
追う

□ **agree** 動 ①同意する ②意見が一
致する agree with（人）に同意する

□ **alive** 熟 come alive 元気になる
keep 〜 alive 〜を生かしておく

□ **all** 熟 after all やはり、結局 all
along 最初からずっと all kinds of
あらゆる種類の all one's life ずっ
と、生まれてから all over 〜中で、全
体に亘って、〜の至る所で all over
one's face 顔一面に all right 大丈
夫で、よろしい、申し分ない、わかっ
た、承知した all the time ずっと、い
つも、その間ずっと all the way ず
っと、はるばる、最後まで all the
way through 十分に、すべて all
together みんなが一緒になって in
all parts of the world 全世界の地
域で not 〜 at all 少しも［全然］〜
ない That's all right. いいんですよ。

□ **allow** 動 ①許す、《– … to 〜》…が
〜するのを可能にする、…に〜させて
おく ②与える

□ **alone** 熟 leave 〜 alone 〜をそっ
としておく

□ **along** 熟 all along 最初からずっ
と along with 〜と一緒に go along
with 〜に同調する play along with
〜と調子を合わせる

□ **aloud** 副 大声で、(聞こえるように)
声を出して

□ **amazing** 形 驚くべき、見事な

WORD LIST

□ **among** 熟 be popular among ~ の間で人気がある

□ **angrily** 副 怒って, 腹立たしげに

□ **announce** 動 (人に)知らせる, 公表する

□ **annoyed** 形 イライラした

□ **any** 熟 any time いつでも not ~ any longer もはや~でない[~しない] not ~ any more もう[これ以上]~ない

□ **anymore** 副 《通例否定文, 疑問文で》今はもう, これ以上, これから

□ **anyone** 代 ①《疑問文・条件節で》誰か ②《否定文で》誰も(~ない) ③《肯定文で》誰でも

□ **anything** 熟 do anything 何でもする more than anything 何よりも

□ **anywhere** 副 どこかへ[に], どこにも, どこへも, どこにでも

□ **apart** 副 ①ばらばらに, 離れて ②別にして, それだけで fall apart 崩れる

□ **ape** 名 類人猿

□ **appear** 動 ①現れる, 見えてくる ②(~のように)見える, ~らしい

□ **appreciate** 動 ①正しく評価する, よさがわかる ②価値[相場]が上がる ③ありがたく思う

□ **argue** 動 ①論じる, 議論する ②主張する

□ **armor** 名 よろい, かぶと, 甲冑 suit of armor 鎧一式

□ **around** 熟 fly around 飛び回る look around まわりを見回す run around 走り回る turn around 振り向く, 向きを変える, 方向転換する walk around 歩き回る, ぶらぶら歩く

□ **arrow** 名 (弓矢の)矢

□ **as** 熟 as a reward for ~に対する報酬として as for ~に関しては, ~はどうかと言うと as good as ~も同然で, ほとんど~ as if あたかも~のように, まるで~みたいに as

long as ~する以上は, ~である限りは as soon as ~するとすぐ, ~するや否や as ~ as one can できる限り ~ as ~ as possible できるだけ ~ just as (ちょうど)であろうとおり the same ~ as …… と同じ(ような)~ twice as good as ~の2倍もよい

□ **ask for** ~を求める ask for forgiveness 許しを乞う

□ **ask ~ if** ~かどうか尋ねる

□ **Aslan** 名 アスラン《キャラクター名》

□ **asleep** 形 眠って(いる状態の) fall asleep 眠り込む, 寝入る

□ **assured** 形 保障された

□ **at** 熟 at first 最初は, 初めのうちは at last ついに, とうとう at once すぐに, 同時に at that moment その時に, その瞬間に at the end of ~の終わりに at the same time 同時に at this これを見て, そこで(すぐに)

□ **attack** 動 ①襲う, 攻める ②非難する ③(病気が)おかす

□ **awake** 形 目が覚めて

□ **away** 熟 far away 遠く離れて from far away 遠くから go away 立ち去る pull away [車が]発車して離れて行く pull away from ~から離れる right away すぐに run away 走り去る, 逃げ出す slip away すり抜ける, こっそり去る, 静かに立ち去る take away ①連れ去る ②取り上げる, 奪い去る ③取り除く take someone away (人)を連れ出す walk away 立ち去る, 遠ざかる wipe ~ away ~を拭い取る

□ **awe** 名 畏敬(の念), 畏怖 in awe 畏敬の念を抱いて look at someone with awe 感心したように(人)の顔を見る

113

B

□ **Bacchus** 名 バッカス, 酒の神

□ **back** 熟 **come back** 戻る **come back to** ～へ帰ってくる, ～に戻る **find one's way back** 元の場所にたどり着く **get back** 戻る, 帰る **get back at someone for** ～のことで (人)に仕返しをする **get ～ back** ～を取り返す[戻す] **go back to ～** に帰る[戻る], ～に遡る, (中断していた作業に)再び取り掛かる **grow back** 成長して元の状態に戻る **look back at** ～に視線を戻す, ～を振り返って見る **push back** 押し返す, 押しのける **take back** ①取り戻す ②(言葉, 約束を)取り消す, 撤回する **turn back** 元に戻る

□ **backward** 副 逆に, 過去にさかのぼって

□ **badger** 名 アナグマ

□ **badly** 副 ①悪く, まずく, へたに ②とても, ひどく

□ **band** 名 ①ひも, 帯 ②楽団, 団 (party) ③縞模様 **band of** ～の集団

□ **banner** 名 旗, 垂れ幕, 大見出し

□ **bargaining** 名 交渉

□ **battle** 名 戦闘, 戦い

□ **battlefield** 名 戦場

□ **batty** 形 少し頭のおかしい

□ **bear** 名 熊

□ **beard** 名 あごひげ

□ **beast** 名 動物, けもの

□ **beat** 動 打つ, 殴打する

□ **beaten** 形 打たれた, 打ち負かされた, 疲れ切った

□ **beaver** 名 ビーバー《動物》

□ **because of** ～のために, ～の理由で

□ **bedtime** 名 就寝の時刻

□ **beer** 名 ビール

□ **before** 熟 **the night before** 前の晩

□ **beg** 動 懇願する, お願いする **I beg your pardon.** ごめんなさい. 失礼ですが. もう一度言ってください.

□ **beginning** 名 初め, 始まり

□ **behind** 前 ①～の後ろに, ～の背後に ②～に遅れて, ～に劣って 副 ①後ろに, 背後に ②遅れて, 劣って

□ **bell** 名 ベル, 鈴, 鐘

□ **beneath** 前 下に, 劣って

□ **bet** 動 きっと～だと確信する

□ **betray** 動 裏切る

□ **better** 熟 **feel better** 気分がよくなる

□ **bit** 名 ①小片, 少量 ②《a–》少し, ちょっと **get a bit sweaty** 少し汗ばむ **have a bit of fun** ちょっとばかり楽しむ **not one bit** 少しも～ない

□ **bite** 動 かむ, かじる

□ **blanket** 名 毛布

□ **blood** 名 血, 血液

□ **blow** 動 ①(風が)吹く, (風が)～を吹き飛ばす ②息を吹く, (鼻を)かむ ③破裂する ④吹奏する **blow into** ～に息を吹き込む

□ **blue-green** 形 青緑色の

□ **bone** 名 骨, 《-s》骨格

□ **bookshelf** 名 本棚

□ **boot** 名 ブーツ, 長靴《通例, boots》 **pull on one's boots** ブーツを履く

□ **both A and B** A も B も

□ **both of them** 彼ら[それら]両方とも

□ **bother** 動 悩ませる

□ **bottom** 名 ①底, 下部, すそ野, ふもと, 最下位, 根底 ②尻

□ **bow** 動 (～に)お辞儀する 名 ①お辞儀, えしゃく ②弓, 弓状のもの

□ **bowl** 名 どんぶり, わん, ボウル

□ **boy** 熟 **my boy** (親しい)友達《呼びかけ》

□ **branch** 名 ①枝 ②支流, 支部

□ **brave** 形 勇敢な

□ **bravely** 副 勇敢に（も）

□ **bravery** 名 勇敢さ, 勇気ある行動

□ **breath** 名 ①息, 呼吸 ②《a－》(風の)そよぎ, 気配, きざし lose one's breath 息切れする out of breath 息を切らして

□ **breathe** 動 ①呼吸する ②ひと息つく, 休息する

□ **bright** 形 明るい

□ **brightly** 副 明るく, 輝いて, 快活に

□ **bring out** (物)をとりだす, 引き出す, (新製品など)を出す

□ **broad** 形 幅の広い

□ **broken down** 《be－》壊れている

□ **bundle** 名 束, 包み, 一巻き

□ **bush** 名 低木の茂み

□ **but** 熟 not ～ but … ～ではなくて… nothing but ただ～だけ, ～にすぎない, ～のほかは何も…ない

□ **butter** 名 バター

□ **by** 熟 by itself ひとりでに by oneself 一人で, 自分だけで, 独力で by the time ～する時までに by then その時までに by this time この時までに, もうすでに close by すぐ近くに go by (時が)過ぎる, 経過する stand by そばに立つ, 傍観する, 待機する

C

□ **C. S. Lewis** C. S. ルイス《著者名》

□ **Cair Paravel** ケアパラヴェル《都と城の名》

□ **call for** ～を求める, 訴える, ～を呼び求める, 呼び出す call for help 助けを求めて呼ぶ

□ **call out** 叫ぶ, 呼び出す, 声を掛ける

□ **call to** ～に声をかける

□ **camp** 名 野営(地), キャンプ

□ **can** 熟 as ～ as one can できる限り Can you ～? ～してくれますか。 can't live without ～なしで生きられない can't wait to ～したくてたまらない

□ **capital** 名 首都 形 首都の

□ **captain** 名 長, 船長, 首領, 主将

□ **care** 熟 not care 構わない take care of ～の世話をする, ～の面倒を見る, ～に対処する

□ **carpet** 名 じゅうたん, 敷物

□ **carry on** 持ち運ぶ

□ **case** 熟 in case ～だといけないので, 念のため, 万が一

□ **catch a cold** 風邪をひく

□ **cave** 名 洞窟

□ **ceiling** 名 天井

□ **celebrate** 動 祝う

□ **celebration** 名 ①祝賀 ②祝典, 儀式

□ **centaur** 名 ケンタウロス

□ **certainly** 副 ①確かに, 必ず ②《返答に用いて》もちろん, そのとおり, 承知しました

□ **chapter** 名 (書物の)章

□ **charge** 動 突進する 名 ①責任 ②告発, 罪, 容疑 in charge of ～を任されて, ～を担当して, ～の責任を負って

□ **chase** 動 ①追跡する, 追い[探し]求める ②追い立てる

□ **check** 動 照合する, 検査する

□ **cheek** 名 頬

□ **cheer** 動 喝采を送る

□ **chest** 名 ①大きな箱, 戸棚, たんす ②金庫 ③胸, 肺

□ **chew** 動 噛み砕く

□ **choke** 動 息が詰まる

□ **Christmas** 名 クリスマス Father Christmas サンタクロース

□ **cinema** 名映画館

□ **circle** 名①円, 円周, 輪 ②循環, 軌道

□ **circling** 形円形に動く

□ **clap** 動(手を)たたく

□ **clear** 動①はっきりさせる ②片づける ③晴れる

□ **climb up onto** ～の上に登る

□ **close** 熟 be close to ～に近い close by すぐ近くに hold someone close (人)をギュッと抱き締める

□ **closely** 副①密接に ②念入りに, 詳しく ③ぴったりと

□ **closet** 名タンス, クローゼット

□ **cold** 熟 catch a cold 風邪をひく go cold ゾッとする, 血の気が引く

□ **come** 熟 come alive 元気になる come and ～しに行く come back 戻る come back to ～へ帰ってくる, ～に戻る come down 下りて来る, 田舎へ来る come in 中にはいる, やってくる come in sight 見えてくる come on いいかげんにしろ, もうよせ, さあ来なさい come out 出てくる, 出掛ける, 姿を現す, 発行される come out from ～から出てくる come out of ～から出てくる, ～をうまく乗り越える come over やって来る come running 飛んでくる, かけつける come through 通り抜ける, 成功する, 期待に沿う come to an end 終わる come true 実現する come up 近づいてくる, 階上に行く, 浮上する, 水面へ上ってくる, 発生する, 芽を出す make someone's wish come true (人)の望みをかなえる

□ **comfortable** 形快適な, 心地いい

□ **company** 熟 enjoy the company of (人)との親交を楽しむ

□ **completely** 副完全に, すっかり

□ **confuse** 動混乱させる

□ **confused** 形困惑した, 混乱した

□ **continue** 動続ける

□ **control** 動①管理[支配]する ②抑制する, コントロールする

□ **conversation** 名会話, 会談 in deep conversation 熱心に話し込んで

□ **cooking** 名料理(法), クッキング

□ **copper** 名銅, 銅貨 形銅の, 銅製の

□ **could** 熟 could have done ～だったかもしれない《仮定法》Could you ～?～してくださいますか。 How could ～?何だって～なんてことがありえようか？ If +《主語》+ could ～できればなあ《仮定法》

□ **count** 動①数える ②(～を…と)みなす ③重要[大切]である count to ～まで数える

□ **countryside** 名地方, 田舎

□ **course** 熟 of course もちろん, 当然

□ **courtyard** 名中庭

□ **cover** 動①覆う, 包む, 隠す ②扱う, (～に)わたる, 及ぶ ③代わりを務める ④補う be covered with ～でおおわれている

□ **cozy** 形居心地がよい, くつろげる

□ **cracking** 形鋭い音を立てて割れる

□ **crawl** 動はう, 腹ばいで進む, ゆっくり進む

□ **cream** 名クリーム

□ **creature** 名生き物

□ **cross over to** ～に越境する

□ **crown** 名①冠 ②《the -》王位 ③頂, 頂上 動〔冠を～に〕載せる

□ **cruel** 形残酷な, 厳しい

□ **cry out** 叫ぶ, 大声を上げる

□ **cupboard** 名戸棚, 食器棚

□ **curl** 名巻き毛, 渦巻状のもの

□ **curly** 形巻き毛の

116

□ **curtsey** 图〔婦人の〕おじぎ

□ **cushion** 图クッション, 座布団

□ **cut down** 切り倒す, 打ちのめす

D

□ **dam** 图ダム

□ **dance to music** 音楽に合わせて踊る

□ **danger** 熟 put someone in danger (人) を危険にさらす

□ **dare** 動あえて～する

□ **day** 熟 one day (過去の) ある日, (未来の) いつか

□ **day and night** 昼も夜も

□ **dear** 熟 Oh, dear あら, まあ

□ **dearie** 图親愛なる人

□ **death** 图①死, 死ぬこと ②《the ‐》終えん, 消滅

□ **decorated** 形装飾 [飾り付け] された

□ **decoration** 图飾り付け, 装飾

□ **dedication** 图装飾

□ **deep** 熟 in deep conversation 熱心に話し込んで

□ **deer** 图シカ (鹿)

□ **defend** 動弁護する

□ **delight** 图喜び, 愉快 Turkish delight ロクム《トルコの伝統菓子, 粉砂糖をまぶしたゼリーあめ》

□ **delighted** 形喜んでいる, うれしそうな delighted with ～を喜んでいる

□ **deliver** 動〔伝言などを〕伝える

□ **describe** 動〔言葉で〕描写する, 特色を述べる, 説明する hard to describe 筆舌に尽くしがたい

□ **dessert** 图デザート

□ **destroy** 動破壊する, 絶滅させる, 無効にする

□ **detail** 图細部, 《-s》詳細

□ **different** 熟 be different from ～と違う in a different way 別の方法で

□ **direction** 图①方向, 方角 ②《-s》指示, 説明書 ③指導, 指揮 in the direction of ～の方向に

□ **dirt** 图①汚れ, 泥, ごみ ②土

□ **disappear** 動見えなくなる, 姿を消す, なくなる

□ **disappointing** 形がっかりさせる

□ **disappointment** 图失望, 落胆

□ **discuss** 動議論 [検討] する

□ **disobey** 動服従しない, 背く

□ **distant** 形①遠い, 隔たった ②よそよそしい, 距離のある in a distant part of ～の遠隔地に

□ **doorknob** 图ドアの取っ手

□ **doubt** 動～を疑う

□ **down** 熟 be broken down 壊れている come down 下りて来る, 田舎へ来る cut down 切り倒す, 打ちのめす down the hall 廊下の先に fall down 落ちる, 転ぶ fall down at on one's face 顔からうつぶせに倒れ込む go down 下に降りる lay down 下に置く, 横たえる let down 期待を裏切る, 失望させる lie down 横になる, 低くする, 下げる look down 見下ろす look down at ～に目 [視線] を落とす put down 下に置く, 下ろす slow down 速度を落とす

□ **drag** 動引きずる

□ **dragon** 图竜, ドラゴン

□ **drinking** 图飲むこと, 飲酒

□ **driver** 图①運転手 ②〔馬車の〕御者

□ **dug** 動 dig (掘る) の過去, 過去分詞

□ **dull** 形鈍い, ぼんやりした

□ **dust** 動ちり [ほこり] を払う dust off 埃を払う

□ **dwarf** 图小人

117

E

- [ ] **each** 熟 each other お互いに hold each other 抱き合う on each side それぞれの側に
- [ ] **eagle** 名 ワシ
- [ ] **eastern** 形 ①東方の, 東向きの ②東洋の, 東洋風の
- [ ] **eat one's fill of** 〜を思う存分食べる
- [ ] **Ed** 名 エド《Edmundの愛称》
- [ ] **Edmund** 名 エドマンド《キャラクター名》
- [ ] **empty** 形 空っぽの, 誰もいない
- [ ] **end** at the end of 〜の終わりに come to an end 終わる
- [ ] **enjoy the company of** (人) との親交を楽しむ
- [ ] **enough** 熟 enough to do 〜するのに十分な have enough 業を煮やす
- [ ] **escape** 動 逃げる, 免れる, もれる
- [ ] **even so** たとえそうであっても
- [ ] **even though** 〜であるけれども, 〜にもかかわらず
- [ ] **every time** 〜するときはいつも
- [ ] **everybody** 代 誰でも, 皆
- [ ] **everyone** 代 誰でも, 皆
- [ ] **everything** 代 すべてのこと[もの], 何でも, 何もかも
- [ ] **everywhere** 副 どこにいても, いたるところに
- [ ] **evil** 形 邪悪な
- [ ] **Ex Traroom** extra roomの聞き間違い
- [ ] **except** 前 〜を除いて, 〜のほかは except for 〜を除いて, 〜がなければ
- [ ] **excited** 形 興奮した, わくわくした
- [ ] **excitedly** 副 興奮して
- [ ] **exciting** 形 刺激的な
- [ ] **exclaim** 動 叫ぶ
- [ ] **exit** 名 出口, 退去
- [ ] **experienced** 形 知識が豊富な
- [ ] **explore** 動 探検[調査]する, 切り開く go exploring 探検に行く
- [ ] **expression** 名 ①表現, 表示, 表情 ②言い回し, 語句
- [ ] **extra** 形 余分の, 臨時の
- [ ] **extreme** 形 最も高い, この上ない
- [ ] **eye** 熟 keep one's eyes open 目を見開いておく look into someone's eyes (人)の目をのぞき込む look someone in the eye (人)の目を直視する with hard eyes 厳しい目つきで

F

- [ ] **face** 熟 all over one's face 顔一面に fall down at on one's face 顔からうつぶせに倒れ込む slap someone across the face (人)の顔を平手打ちする
- [ ] **fact** 熟 in fact つまり, 実は, 要するに
- [ ] **fade** 動 衰える, 弱まる
- [ ] **faint** 動 気絶する
- [ ] **fair** 形 正しい, 公平[正当]な
- [ ] **fairy** 名 妖精 fairy tale おとぎ話
- [ ] **fall** 熟 fall apart 崩れる fall asleep 眠り込む, 寝入る fall down 落ちる, 転ぶ fall down at on one's face 顔からうつぶせに倒れ込む fall on 〜に降りかかる fall out 落ちる, 飛び出す fall out of 〜から転げ落ちる fall over 〜につまずく, 〜の上に倒れかかる
- [ ] **fallen** 動 fall (落ちる)の過去分詞
- [ ] **false** 形 うその, 間違った, にせの, 不誠実な make a false step 足を踏み外す
- [ ] **familiar** 形 聞き覚えのある

118

□ **far away** 遠く離れて **from far away** 遠くから

□ **farther** 副 もっと遠く，さらに先に

□ **Father Christmas** サンタクロース

□ **fault** 名 落ち度

□ **faun** 名 フォーン《半人半羊の林野牧畜の神（ローマ神話）》

□ **fear** 動 ①恐れる ②心配する

□ **fearful** 形 ①恐ろしい ②心配な，気づかって

□ **fearsome** 形 恐ろしい

□ **feather** 名 羽，《-s》羽毛

□ **feel better** 気分がよくなる

□ **feel like** ～がほしい，～したい気がする，～のような感じがする

□ **feel sick** 気分が悪い

□ **feeling** 動 feel（感じる）の現在分詞 名 ①感じ，気持ち ②触感，知覚 ③同情，思いやり，感受性 形 感じる，感じやすい，情け深い

□ **fellow** 名 仲間

□ **female** 形 女性の，婦人の，雌の

□ **few** 熟 **take a few steps forward** 数歩前に出る

□ **field** 名 野原，戦場

□ **fighter** 名 戦う人，戦士

□ **fighting** 名 戦闘

□ **fill** 熟 **be filled with** ～でいっぱいになる **eat one's fill of** ～を思う存分食べる

□ **find one's way back** 元の場所にたどり着く

□ **find oneself in** 気がつくと～にいる

□ **fine** 形 上質の

□ **finish doing** ～するのを終える

□ **finished** 動 finish（終わる）の過去，過去分詞 形 ①終わった，仕上がった ②洗練された ③もうだめになった

□ **fire** 名 炉火 **light a fire** 火をつける

□ **firelight** 名 〔暖炉などの〕火明り

□ **first** 熟 **at first** 最初は，初めのうちは

□ **fisherman** 名 漁師，（趣味の）釣り人

□ **fishermen** 名 fisherman（漁師）の複数

□ **fishing** 名 釣り，漁業 形 釣りの，漁業の **fishing rod** 釣りざお

□ **flap** 動 羽ばたきする

□ **flat** 形 ①平らな ②しぼんだ，空気の抜けた 副 ①平らに，平たく ②きっかり 名 ①平面，平地 ②アパート

□ **flesh** 名 肉，表皮

□ **flute** 名 フルート《楽器》

□ **fly around** 飛び回る

□ **fly to** ～まで飛行機で行く

□ **foggy** 形 霧がかかった

□ **followed by** 《be－》その後に～が続いて

□ **follower** 名 追随者

□ **following** 動 follow（ついていく）の現在分詞 形 《the－》次の，次に続く **following week** 翌週

□ **fool** 名 愚か者

□ **foot** 名 **on foot** 歩いて

□ **footprint** 名 足跡

□ **footstep** 名 足音

□ **for** 熟 **for a long time** 長い間 **for a moment** 少しの間 **for a while** しばらくの間，少しの間 **for fun** 楽しみで **for long** 長い間 **for oneself** 独力で，自分のために **for ～ years** ～年間，～年にわたって

□ **forget to do** ～することを忘れる

□ **forgive** 動 許す

□ **forgiveness** 名 許す（こと），寛容 **ask for forgiveness** 許しを乞う

□ **fork** 名 フォーク

□ **fortunately** 副 幸運にも

□ **forward** 副 前方に　**look forward to** 〜を期待する　**take a few steps forward** 数歩前に出る

□ **fox** 名 キツネ（狐）

□ **freezing** 形 酷寒の，こごえるような

□ **friend** 名 **make friends with** 〜と友達になる

□ **friendly** 形 信頼できる

□ **frightening** 形 恐ろしい

□ **front** 熟 **in front of** 〜の前に，〜の正面に

□ **frozen** 動 freeze（凍る）の過去分詞

□ **frying pan** フライパン

□ **full of** 《be −》〜で一杯である

□ **fun** 名 **for fun** 楽しみで　**have a bit of fun** ちょっとばかり楽しむ　**have fun** 楽しむ　**just for fun** 単なるお遊びで

□ **funny** 形 ①おもしろい，こっけいな ②奇妙な，うさんくさい

□ **funny-looking** 形 変な格好の，変わった形の

□ **fur** 名 毛，毛皮（製品）

□ **further** 副 いっそう遠く，その上に，もっと

G

□ **gather** 動 ①集まる，集める ②生じる，増す ③推測する

□ **genie** 名 精霊，悪霊

□ **gentle** 形 ①優しい，温和な ②柔らかな

□ **gently** 副 親切に，上品に，そっと，優しく

□ **geography** 名 地理，地理学

□ **get** 熟 **get a bit sweaty** 少し汗ばむ　**get back** 戻る，帰る　**get 〜 back** 〜を取り返す［戻す］　**get back at someone for** 〜のことで（人）に仕

返しをする　**get going** ①急ぐ ②出かける，出発する　**get hurt** けがをする　**get in** 中に入る，乗り込む　**get in trouble** 厄介ごと［トラブル・面倒なこと］に入る，入り込む，〜に巻き込まれる　**get near** 接近する　**get off**（〜から）降りる　**get off of** 〜から離れる　**get on**（電車などに）乗る，気が合う　**get out of** 〜から外へ出る［抜け出る］　**get ready** 用意［支度］をする　**get rid of** 〜を取り除く　**get serious** 真面目になる　**get there** そこに到着する，目的を達成する，成功する　**get tired** 疲れる　**get to**（事）を始める，〜に達する［到着する］　**get up** 起き上がる，立ち上がる　**get worse** 悪化する

□ **ghost** 名 幽霊

□ **giant** 名 巨人，大男

□ **give a reward to** 〜に報酬を与える

□ **give one's life** 命を犠牲にする

□ **give someone a hug**（人）を抱き締める

□ **give up** あきらめる，やめる，引き渡す

□ **glad to do** 《be −》〜してうれしい，喜んで〜する

□ **go** 熟 **go after** 〜の後を追う　**go along with** 〜に同調する　**go and** 〜しに行く　**go away** 立ち去る　**go back to** 〜に帰る［戻る］，〜に遡る，（中断していた作業に）再び取り掛かる　**go by**（時が）過ぎる，経過する　**go cold** ゾッとする，血の気が引く　**go doing** 〜をしに行く　**go down** 下に降りる　**go exploring** 探検に行く　**go for** 〜に出かける，〜を追い求める，〜を好む　**go home** 帰宅する　**go into** 〜に入る，（仕事）に就く　**go off** ①出かける，去る，出発する ②始める，突然〜し出す ③（電気）が消える　**go off to** 〜に向かう　**go on** 続く，続ける，進み続ける　**go out** 外出する，外へ出る　**go past** 〜を通り過ぎる　**go through** 通り抜ける，一つずつ順番

に検討する **go to sleep** 寝る **go to work** 仕事に取りかかる **go with** 〜と一緒に行く **let someone go** (人)を行かせてやる **where to go** 行くべき所

□ **goat** 图ヤギ(山羊)

□ **godfather** 图男性の名付け親

□ **going** 熟get going ①急ぐ ②出かける, 出発する

□ **gold** 图金, 金製品

□ **golden** 形①金色の ②金製の

□ **gone** 形なくなった

□ **good** 熟as good as 〜も同然で, ほとんど〜 **good nose** 嗅覚の優れた鼻 **twice as good as** 〜の2倍もよい

□ **good-bye** 間さようなら

□ **goodness** 熟Oh, my goodness! 何てことだ!, 大変だ!

□ **gotten** 動get(得る)の過去分詞

□ **grand** 形壮大な

□ **grass** 图草, 牧草(地), 芝生

□ **ground** 熟on the ground 地面に **roll on the ground** 地面を転げる

□ **grow back** 成長して元の状態に戻る

□ **grow up** 成長する, 大人になる

□ **guard** 動守る, 監視する

□ **guest** 图客, ゲスト

H

□ **ha** 間ほう, まあ, おや《驚き・悲しみ・不満・喜び・笑い声などを表す》

□ **halfway** 副途中で

□ **hall** 图公会堂, ホール, 大広間, 玄関 **down the hall** 廊下の先に

□ **ham** 图ハム

□ **hand** 熟knock 〜 out of someone's hand (人)の手から〜をたたき落とす **reach out a hand** 手

を伸ばす **shake someone's hand** (人)の手を握る

□ **handkerchief** 图ハンカチ

□ **hang** 動かかる, かける, つるす, ぶら下がる **hang on** 〜につかまる, しがみつく, がんばる

□ **happen to** たまたま〜する, 偶然〜する

□ **happy** 熟be happy to do 〜してうれしい, 喜んで〜する **not happy about** いい顔をしない

□ **hard** 熟hard to 〜し難い **hard to describe** 筆舌に尽くしがたい **with hard eyes** 厳しい目つきで

□ **hardly** 副ほとんど〜ない

□ **harm** 動危害を加える

□ **hate** 動嫌う, 憎む, (〜するのを)いやがる

□ **have** 熟could have done 〜だったかもしれない《仮定法》 **have a bit of fun** ちょっとばかり楽しむ **have been to** 〜へ行ったことがある **have enough** 業を煮やす **have fun** 楽しむ **never have done** 1度も〜したことがない **will have done** 〜してしまっているだろう《未来完了形》

□ **head** 熟nod one's head うなずく **one's head hung low** うなだれて

□ **heal** 動いえる, いやす, 治る, 治す

□ **hear about** 〜について聞く

□ **hear of** 〜について聞く

□ **he-beaver** 图雄のビーバー

□ **help** 熟call for help 助けを求めて呼ぶ **help 〜 with** ……を〜の面で手伝う

□ **here** 熟here is 〜 こちらは〜です。 **over here** こっちへ[に]；ほら, さあ《人の注意を引く》

□ **hey** 間①《呼びかけ・注意を促して》おい, ちょっと ②へえ, おや, まあ

□ **hidden** 動hide(隠れる)の過去分詞 形隠れた, 秘密の **stay hidden** 隠れたままでいる

□ **hide** 動 隠れる, 隠す, 隠れて見えない, 秘密にする **play hide and seek** かくれんぼをして遊ぶ

□ **hiding place** 隠れ場所

□ **High King** 上級王

□ **high spirit** 不屈の精神

□ **high treason** (国家や君主に対する)反逆, 大逆

□ **hold each other** 抱き合う

□ **hold someone close** (人)をギュッと抱き締める

□ **hold up** 〜を持ち上げる

□ **holly** 名 モチノキ, ヒイラギ(柊)

□ **home** 熟 **go home** 帰宅する

□ **honest** 形 正直な, ごまかしがない

□ **hood** 名 フード, ずきん

□ **hopelessly** 副 絶望して, 救いようがなく

□ **horn** 名 (牛・羊などの)角, 角材, (楽器の)ホルン

□ **horrible** 形 恐ろしい

□ **host** 名 客をもてなす主人

□ **housekeeper** 名 家政婦

□ **how** 熟 **How could 〜?** 何だって〜なんてことがありえようか? **how to 〜する方法 tell 〜 how to … 〜**に…のやり方を教える

□ **however** 接 けれども, だが

□ **hug** 名 抱き締めること **give someone a hug** (人)を抱き締める

□ **huge** 形 巨大な

□ **hundreds of** 何百もの〜

□ **hung** 熟 **one's head hung low** うなだれて

□ **hunting** 名 狩り

□ **hurt** 熟 **get hurt** けがをする

I

□ **icy** 形 氷で覆われた

□ **idea** 熟 **The very idea!** とんでもない!

□ **if** 熟 **ask 〜 if** 〜かどうか尋ねる **If +《主語》+ could 〜** できればなあ《仮定法》 **as if** あたかも〜のように, まるで〜みたいに **if only** 〜でありさえすれば **see if** 〜かどうかを確かめる **what if** もし〜だったらどうなるだろうか **wonder if** 〜ではないかと思う

□ **ignore** 動 無視する

□ **imagine** 動 想像する, 心に思い描く

□ **immediately** 副 すぐに, 〜するやいなや

□ **impossible** 形 あり得ない

□ **in** 熟 **in a different way** 別の方法で **in a distant part of** 〜の遠隔地に **in a kind way** 優しく **in a moment** ただちに **in all parts of the world** 全世界の地域で **in an instant** たちまち, ただちに **in awe** 畏敬の念を抱いて **in case** 〜だといけないので, 念のため, 万が一 **in charge of** 〜を任されて, 〜を担当して, 〜の責任を負って **in deep conversation** 熱心に話し込んで **in fact** つまり, 実は, 要するに **in front of** 〜の前に, 〜の正面に **in just a moment** 〔それから〕すぐに **in quite** かなり **in reply** 返答として **in response** それに応じて **in sight** 視野に入って **in the direction of** 〜の方向に **in the middle of** 〜の真ん中[中ほど]に **in the world** 世界で **in this way** このようにして **in trouble** 面倒な状況で, 困って

□ **incredible** 形 信じられないほど素晴らしい

□ **instant** 名 瞬間, 寸時 **in an instant** たちまち, ただちに

□ **instead** 副 その代わりに **instead of** 〜の代わりに, 〜をしないで, 〜ではなくて

□ **interested** 形 興味を持った, 関心のある

☐ **iron** 形鉄の, 鉄製の

☐ **it** 名 (鬼ごっこなどの) 鬼

☐ **It is ～ for someone to ...** (人) が…するのは～だ

☐ **It takes someone ～ to ...** (人) が…するのに～ (時間など) がかかる

☐ **itself** 代それ自体, それ自身 **by itself** ひとりでに

J

☐ **jingling** 形チリンチリンと鳴る

☐ **joy** 名喜び, 楽しみ

☐ **jump on** ～に飛びかかる

☐ **jump over** ～の上を飛び越える

☐ **jump up** 素早く立ち上がる

☐ **junior** 形若手の

☐ **just** 熟 **in just a moment** 〔それから〕すぐに **just as** (ちょうど) であろうとおり **just for fun** 単なるお遊びで **just then** そのとたんに

K

☐ **keep** 熟 **keep off** 防ぐ **keep one's eyes open** 目を見開いておく **keep one's mind on** ～に集中する **keep one's promise** 約束を守る **keep quiet about** ～について黙っている **keep someone from** ～から (人) を阻む **keep ～ a secret from** ～を (人) に秘密にしておく **keep ～ alive** ～を生かしておく

☐ **kettle** 名なべ, やかん

☐ **kidnap** 動誘拐する

☐ **kind** 熟 **all kinds of** あらゆる種類の **in a kind way** 優しく **kind of** ある程度, いくらか, ～のようなもの 〔人〕

☐ **kind-looking** 形親切そうな

☐ **kindly** 副親切に, 優しく

☐ **kiss** 動キスする

☐ **kitty** 名 (子) 猫 (ちゃん)

☐ **knee** 名ひざ

☐ **knife** 名ナイフ, 小刀, 包丁, 短剣

☐ **knight** 名騎士 (の称号)

☐ **knives** 名knife (ナイフ) の複数

☐ **knock** 動ノックする, たたく, ぶつける **knock ～ out of someone's hand** (人) の手から～をたたき落とす

☐ **known to** 《be－》～に知られている

L

☐ **laid** 動lay (置く) の過去, 過去分詞

☐ **lamppost** 名街灯

☐ **last** 熟 **at last** ついに, とうとう

☐ **laugh** 熟 **with a laugh** 笑いながら

☐ **laughing** 形笑っている

☐ **lay** 動①置く, 横たえる, 敷く ②整える ③卵を産む ④lie (横たわる) の過去 **lay down** 下に置く, 横たえる

☐ **lean** 動①もたれる, 寄りかかる ②傾く, 傾ける **lean over** ～に身を乗り出す, ～にかがみ込む

☐ **leave ～ alone** ～をそっとしておく

☐ **led** 動lead (導く) の過去, 過去分詞

☐ **legend** 名伝説, 伝説的人物, 言い伝え

☐ **leopard** 名ヒョウ

☐ **let down** 期待を裏切る, 失望させる

☐ **let out** (声を) 出す, 発する

☐ **let someone go** (人) を行かせてやる

☐ **let us** どうか私たちに～させてください

123

☐ **liar** 图 うそつき

☐ **library** 图 書斎, 書庫

☐ **lie** 動 嘘をつく **lie down** 横になる, 低くする, 下げる **tell a lie** うそをつく

☐ **life** 图 **all one's life** ずっと, 生まれてから **give one's life** 命を犠牲にする **return to life** 生き返る

☐ **lift** 動 持ち上げる, 上がる

☐ **light a fire** 火をつける

☐ **like** 熟 **Would you like ~?** ~はいかがですか。 **act like an adult** 大人のように行動する **feel like** ~がほしい, ~したい気がする, ~のような感じがする **like this** このような, こんなふうに **look like** ~のように見える, ~に似ている **sound like** ~のように聞こえる **would like to** ~したいと思う

☐ **lip** 图 唇, 《-s》口

☐ **liquid** 图 液体

☐ **lit** 動 light (火をつける) の過去, 過去分詞

☐ **live** 熟 **Long live ~!** ~万歳! **can't live without** ~なしで生きられない

☐ **logic** 图 論理 (学), 理屈 **matter of logic** 論理的な問題

☐ **London** 图 ロンドン《英国の首都》

☐ **long** 熟 **Long live ~!** ~万歳! **as long as** ~する以上は, ~である限りは **for a long time** 長い間 **for long** 長い間 **long way** はるかに

☐ **longer** 熟 **no longer** もはや~でない[~しない] **not ~ any longer** もはや~でない[~しない]

☐ **look** 熟 **look around** まわりを見回す **look at someone with awe** 感心したように (人) の顔を見る **look back at** ~に視線を戻す, ~を振り返って見る **look down** 見下ろす **look down at** ~に目 [視線] を落とす **look for** ~を探す **look forward to** ~を期待する **look in** 中を見る,

立ち寄る **look into** ①~を検討する, ~を研究する ②~の中を見る, ~をのぞき込む **look into someone's eyes** (人) の目をのぞき込む **look like** ~のように見える, ~に似ている **look out** ①外を見る ②気をつける, 注意する **look over at** ~の方を見る **look someone in the eye** (人) の目を直視する **look strangely at** 怪訝な顔で~を見る **look to** ~しようとする **look up** 見上げる **look up to** ~を仰ぎ見る

☐ **lose one's breath** 息切れする

☐ **lost** 形 道に迷った

☐ **lot of** 熟 《a-》たくさんの~

☐ **loudly** 副 大声で, 騒がしく

☐ **lovely** 形 すてきな

☐ **loving** 形 愛する, 愛情のこもった

☐ **low** 熟 **one's head hung low** うなだれて

☐ **lower** 形 もっと低い, 下級の, 劣った

☐ **Lu** 图 ルー《Lucyの愛称》

☐ **lucky for** (人) にとってラッキーだったことには

☐ **Lucy** 图 ルーシー《キャラクター名》

☐ **Lucy Barfield** ルーシー・バーフィールド《人名》

☐ **lying** 動 lie (うそをつく・横たわる) の現在分詞

M

☐ **machine** 熟 **sewing machine** ミシン

☐ **mad** 形 気が狂って **mad at** ~に対して腹を立てる

☐ **magic** 图 ①魔法, 手品 ②魔力 形 魔法の, 魔力のある

☐ **magical** 形 ①魔法の力による ②魅惑的な

☐ **main** 形 主な, 主要な

- [ ] **Majesty** 名 陛下 **your Majesty** 陛下

- [ ] **make** 熟 **make a false step** 足を踏み外す **make a noise** 物音を立てる, 騒ぐ **make a sign to** 〜するように合図する **make friends with** 〜と友達になる **make noise** 音を立てる **make sense** うなずける, 理にかなう **make someone upset** (人) を動揺させる **make someone's wish come true** (人) の望みをかなえる **make up** 作り出す, 考え出す, 〜を構成 [形成] する **make up a story** 作り話をする

- [ ] **many** 熟 **so many** 非常に多くの

- [ ] **mark** 名 印, 記号, 跡

- [ ] **marking** 名 マーク, 目印, 模様

- [ ] **marmalade** 名 マーマレード

- [ ] **marry** 動 結婚する

- [ ] **match** 名 マッチ (棒)

- [ ] **matter** 熟 **a matter of** 〜の問題 **matter of logic** 論理的な問題 **no matter what** たとえどんな〜であろうと **not matter** どうでもいい, 問題にならない

- [ ] **Maugrim** 名 モーグリム《キャラクター名》

- [ ] **May I 〜?** 〜してもよいですか。

- [ ] **mean** 形 意地悪な 熟 **I do not mean to** 〜するつもりはないのですが **I mean** つまり, と言うか **not mean to** 〜するつもりはない

- [ ] **meaning** 名 ①意味, 趣旨 ②重要性

- [ ] **meanly** 副 卑劣に

- [ ] **meanwhile** 副 その間に

- [ ] **meet** 熟 **nice to meet you** お会いできてうれしい

- [ ] **melt** 動 溶ける, 溶かす

- [ ] **melting** 名 雪解け 形 溶ける

- [ ] **memory** 名 記憶 (力), 思い出

- [ ] **merry** 形 陽気な, 愉快な, 快活な

- [ ] **metal** 名 金属, 合金

- [ ] **mice** 名 mouse (ネズミ) の複数

- [ ] **middle** 名 中間, 最中 **in the middle of** 〜の真ん中 [中ほど] に

- [ ] **might** 助《mayの過去》①〜かもしれない ②〜してもよい, 〜できる

- [ ] **mighty** 形 強大な

- [ ] **mind** 名 ①心, 精神, 考え ②知性 **keep one's mind on** 〜に集中する 動 ①気にする, いやがる ②気をつける, 用心する

- [ ] **mine** 名 鉱山

- [ ] **mirror** 名 鏡

- [ ] **missing** 形 行方不明の

- [ ] **mission** 名 使命, 任務

- [ ] **modestly** 副 控えめに, 謙遜して

- [ ] **moment** 名 ①瞬間, ちょっとの間 ②(特定の) 時, 時期 **at that moment** その時に, その瞬間に **for a moment** 少しの間 **in a moment** ただちに **in just a moment** 〔それから〕すぐに

- [ ] **monster** 名 非道な人

- [ ] **mood** 名 気分, 機嫌, 雰囲気, 憂うつ

- [ ] **moonlight** 名 月明かり, 月光

- [ ] **more** 熟 **more and more** ますます **more of** 〜よりもっと **more than** 〜以上 **more than anything** 何よりも **no more** もう〜ない **not 〜 any more** もう [これ以上] 〜ない **some more** もう少し

- [ ] **moss** 名 コケ《植物》

- [ ] **most of the way** ほとんど

- [ ] **mostly** 副 主として, 多くは, ほとんど

- [ ] **motion** 名 ①運動, 移動 ②身振り, 動作

- [ ] **move on** 先に進む

- [ ] **movement** 名 ①動き, 運動 ②《-s》行動 ③引っ越し ④変動

- [ ] **moving** 動 move (動く) の現在分詞 形 ①動いている ②感動させる

125

A
B
C
D
E
F
G
H
I
J
K
L
M
N
O
P
Q
R
S
T
U
V
W
X
Y
Z

□ **much** 熟 too much 過度の

□ **muffler** 名 マフラー, えり巻き

□ **music** 熟 dance to music 音楽に合わせて踊る

□ **my boy** (親しい) 友達《呼びかけ》

□ **my word** これは驚いた

□ **myth** 名 神話

N

□ **Narnia** 名 ナルニア国

□ **near** 熟 get near 接近する

□ **nearby** 副 すぐ近くに

□ **nearly** 副 ①近くに, 親しく ②ほとんど, あやうく

□ **neither A nor B** A と B のどちらも～ない

□ **never have done** 一度も～したことがない

□ **news** 名 報道, ニュース, 便り, 知らせ

□ **next time** 次回に

□ **next to** ～のとなりに, ～の次に

□ **nice to meet you** お会いできてうれしい

□ **night** 熟 day and night 昼も夜も the night before 前の晩

□ **nightmare** 名 悪夢

□ **no longer** もはや～でない[～しない]

□ **no matter what** たとえどんな～であろうと

□ **no more** もう～ない

□ **no one** 誰も [一人も] ～ない

□ **nod** 動 うなずく, うなずいて～を示す nod one's head うなずく

□ **noise** 名 騒音, 騒ぎ, 物音 make a noise 物音を立てる, 騒ぐ make noise 音を立てる

□ **none** 代 (～の) 何も [誰も・少しも]

…ない

□ **nor** 接 ～もまたない neither A nor B A と B のどちらも～ない

□ **normal** 形 普通の, 平均の, 標準的な

□ **northeast** 名 北東, 北東部

□ **nose** 熟 good nose 嗅覚の優れた鼻

□ **not** I do not mean to ～するつもりはないのですが not care 構わない not happy about いい顔をしない not matter どうでもいい, 問題にならない not mean to ～するつもりはない not one bit 少しも～ない not … without ～ing …せずには…しない, ～すれば必ず…する not ～ any longer もはや～でない[～しない] not ～ any more もう[これ以上]～ない not ～ at all 少しも[全然]～ない not ～ but … ～ではなくて…

□ **nothing but** ただ～だけ, ～にすぎない, ～のほかは何も…ない

□ **notice** 動 気がつく, 認める

□ **now** 熟 now that 今や～だから, ～からには right now 今すぐに right now 今すぐに, たった今 up to now 今まで

□ **nymph** 名 ニンフ, 精霊, 妖精

O

□ **oak** 形 オーク (材) の

□ **of course** もちろん, 当然

□ **off** 熟 dust off 埃を払う get off (～から) 降りる get off of ～から離れる go off ①出かける, 去る, 出発する ②始める, 突然～しだす ③ (電気が) 消える go off to ～に向かう keep off 防ぐ pick off ～をもぎとる push off 去る, 帰る rush off 急いで出て行く start off 出発する take off (衣服を) 脱ぐ, 取り去る, ～を取り除く

□ **offer** 動 提案する

WORD LIST

□ **Oh, dear** あら，まあ

□ **ok** 形《許可・同意・満足などを表して。O.K. とも》よろしい，正しい

□ **on** 熟《carry on 持ち運ぶ come on いいかげんにしろ，もうよせ，さあ来なさい fall on 〜に降りかかる get on（電車などに）乗る，気が合う go on 続く，続ける，進み続ける hang on 〜につかまる，しがみつく，がんばる，（電話を）切らずに待つ jump on 〜に飛びかかる move on 先に進む on each side それぞれの側に on foot 歩いて on one's way〔目的地への〕途中にいる on the ground 地面に on the side of 〜を味方に on top of 〜の上（部）に pull on 〜を引っ張る，身につける put on ①〜を身につける，着る ②〜を…の上に置く send someone on（人）を〜に送り出す sit on 〜の上にある，〜の上に乗る，〜の上に乗って動けないようにする spit on 〜に唾を吐きかける walk on 歩き続ける

□ **once** 熟 at once すぐに，同時に

□ **one** 熟 no one 誰も［一人も］〜ない not one bit 少しも〜ない one day（過去の）ある日，（未来の）いつか one of 〜の1つ［人］ one side 片側 this one これ，こちら

□ **onion** 名 タマネギ

□ **only** 熟 if only 〜でありさえすれば

□ **onto** 前 〜の上へ［に］

□ **open** 熟 keep one's eyes open 目を見開いておく

□ **or so** 〜かそこらで

□ **order** 動 命令する

□ **organize** 動〔組織を〕編成する

□ **other** 熟 each other お互いに hold each other 抱き合う

□ **out** 熟 bring out（物）をとりだす，引き出す，（新製品など）を出す call out 叫ぶ，呼び出す，声を掛ける come out 出てくる，出掛ける，姿を現す，発行される come out from 〜から出てくる come out of 〜から出てくる，〜をうまく乗り越える cry out 叫ぶ，大声を上げる fall out 落ちる，飛び出す fall out of 〜から転げ落ちる get out of 〜から外へ出る［抜け出る］go out 外出する，外へ出る knock 〜 out of someone's hand（人）の手から〜をたたき落とす let out（声を）出す，発する look out ①外を見る ②気をつける，注意する out of ①〜から外へ，〜から抜け出して ②〜の範囲外に，〜から離れて ③（ある数）の中から out of breath 息を切らして out of sight 見えないところに pop out 急に飛び出る pull out 引き抜く，引き出す，取り出す put out 外に出す，（手など）を（差し）出す reach out a hand 手を伸ばす run out of 〜から駆け出す run out of a room 部屋から駆け出して行く stay out of the way ちょっかいを出さない step out into 〜に踏み出す，〜に出ていく step out of 〜から出る

□ **oven** 名 かまど，天火，オーブン

□ **over** 形 終わって 熟 all over 〜中で，全体に亘って，〜の至る所で all over one's face 顔一面に be over 終わる come over やって来る cross over to 〜に越境する fall over 〜につまづく，〜の上に倒れかかる jump over 〜の上を飛び越える lean over 〜に身を乗り出す，〜にかがみ込む look over at 〜の方を見る over here こっちへ［に］；ほら，さあ《人の注意を引く》over there あそこに roll 〜 over 〜を転がす step over またぐ take over 引き継ぐ，支配する，乗っ取る walk over 〜の方に歩いていく

□ **owl** 名 フクロウ（梟），ミミズク

P

□ **pack** 動 包む，まとめる

□ **paid** 動 pay（払う）の過去，過去分詞

127

□ **painful** 形 ①痛い, 苦しい, 痛ましい ②骨の折れる, 困難な

□ **palace** 名宮殿, 大邸宅

□ **pale** 形 (色が)薄い, おぼろげな

□ **pan** 名平なべ, フライパン **frying pan** フライパン

□ **pardon** 熟 **I beg your pardon.** ごめんなさい。失礼ですが。もう一度言ってください。 **pardon me** 失礼ですが

□ **parent** 名《-s》両親

□ **part** 熟 **in a distant part of** ~の遠隔地に **in all parts of the world** 全世界の地域で

□ **partly** 副一部分は, ある程度は

□ **past** 前《時間・場所》~を過ぎて, ~を越して **go past** ~を通り過ぎる **walk past** 通り過ぎる

□ **pat** 動軽くたたく

□ **path** 名 ①(踏まれてできた)小道, 歩道 ②進路, 通路

□ **patiently** 副辛抱強く

□ **paw** 名〔動物の爪のある〕足, 手

□ **peacock** 名孔雀

□ **pelican** 名ペリカン

□ **Peter** 名ピーター《キャラクター名》

□ **pick off** ~をもぎとる

□ **pick up** 拾い上げる **pick up a scent** 匂いに気付く

□ **piece** 熟 **split into two pieces** 二つに分割される

□ **pile** 動積み重ねる, 積もる

□ **pipe** 名管, 筒, パイプ

□ **pity** 名哀れみ, 同情, 残念なこと

□ **plan to** ~するつもりである

□ **plate** 名 (浅い)皿

□ **play along with** ~と調子を合わせる

□ **play hide and seek** かくれんぼをして遊ぶ

□ **pleasant** 形心地よい

□ **pleased** 形うれしい

□ **pleasure** 名喜び, 楽しみ, 満足, 娯楽

□ **plenty** 名十分, たくさん, 豊富 **plenty of** たくさんの~ **with plenty of** たくさんの~

□ **plum** 名セイヨウスモモ, プラム

□ **point toward** ~の方を指さす

□ **politely** 副丁寧に

□ **pony** 名ポニー, 小型の馬

□ **poor** 形かわいそうな

□ **pop** 動飛び出させる, 前に突き出す **pop out** 急に飛び出る

□ **popular among** 熟《be – 》~の間で人気がある

□ **possibility** 名可能性, 見込み, 将来性

□ **possible** 形 ①可能な ②ありうる, 起こりうる **as ~ as possible** できるだけ~

□ **pour** 動 ①注ぐ, 浴びせる ②流れ出る, 流れ込む

□ **powdered** 形粉になった, 粉末の

□ **praise** 動ほめる, 賞賛する

□ **prepare for** ~の準備をする

□ **pretend** 動~のふりをする

□ **pretty** 形すてきな

□ **prince** 名王子, プリンス

□ **prisoner** 名囚人, 捕虜 **take someone prisoner** (人)を人質に取る

□ **probably** 副たぶん, あるいは

□ **professor** 名教授, 師匠

□ **promise** 熟 **keep one's promise** 約束を守る

□ **proudly** 副 ①誇らしげに ②うぬぼれて

□ **pudding** 名プディング

□ **pull** 熟 **pull away** 〔車が〕発車して離れて行く **pull away from** ~から離れる **pull on** ~を引っ張る, 身に

つける **pull on one's boots** ブーツ
を履く **pull out** 引き抜く, 引き出す,
取り出す **pull up** 引っ張り上げる

□ **pure** 形 ①純粋な, 混じりけのない
②罪のない, 清い

□ **push back** 押し返す, 押しのける

□ **push off** 去る, 帰る

□ **push one's way through** ～
を押し分けて進む

□ **put** 熟 **put down** 下に置く, 下ろ
す **put in** ～の中に入れる **put on**
①～を身につける, 着る ②～を…の
上に置く **put out** 外に出す, (手な
ど)を(差し)出す **put someone in
danger** (人)を危険にさらす **put up**
～を上げる

Q

□ **queen** 名 女王, 王妃

□ **quickly** 副 敏速に, 急いで

□ **quiet** 熟 **keep quiet about** ～につ
いて黙っている

□ **quietly** 副 ①静かに ②平穏に, 控
えめに

□ **quite** 副 かなり **in quite** かなり

R

□ **rabbit** 名 ウサギ

□ **race** 動 大急ぎで走る

□ **racehorse** 名 競走馬, 競馬馬

□ **raise** 動 〔手などを〕上げる

□ **reach** 動 達する, 手が届く **reach
out a hand** 手を伸ばす

□ **ready** 熟 **be ready to** すぐに〔い
つでも〕～できる, ～する構えで **get
ready** 用意〔支度〕をする

□ **realize** 動 理解する, 実現する

□ **reddish-orange** 形 赤みがかっ
たオレンジ色の

□ **regular** 形 ①規則的な, 秩序のあ
る ②定期的な, 一定の, 習慣的

□ **reindeer** 名 トナカイ

□ **relief** 名 安堵(の気持ち)

□ **remind** 動 思い出させる, 気づかせ
る **remind A of B** AにBのことを連
想させる

□ **repair** 動 修理[修繕]する

□ **repeat** 動 繰り返す

□ **reply** 動 答える, 返事をする, 応答
する 名 答え, 返事, 応答 **in reply** 返
答として

□ **rescue** 動 救う 名 救助, 救出

□ **respect** 動 尊敬[尊重]する

□ **response** 名 応答, 反応, 返答 **in
response** それに応じて

□ **return to life** 生き返る

□ **reward** 名 報酬, 償い, 応報 **as a
reward for** ～に対する報酬として
give a reward to ～に報酬を与える

□ **rid** 動 取り除く **get rid of** ～を取り
除く

□ **right** 形 正しい, 合っている **all
right** 大丈夫で, よろしい, 申し分な
い, わかった, 承知した **right away**
すぐに **right now** 今すぐに **right
now** 今すぐに, たった今 **set things
right** 状況を正常な状態にする
That's all right. いいんですよ。

□ **risk** 動 〔～の〕危険を冒す

□ **roar** 動 ①ほえる ②(人が)わめく
③鳴り響く 名 ①ほえ声, 怒号 ②大
笑い

□ **robe** 名 ローブ, 化粧着, 部屋着

□ **robin** 名 コマドリ《鳥》

□ **rod** 名 棒, さお **fishing rod** 釣りざ
お

□ **rode** 動 ride (乗る)の過去

□ **roll** 動 ①転がる, 転がす ②(波など
が)うねる, 横揺れする ③(時が)た
つ **roll on the ground** 地面を転げ
る **roll ～ over** ～を転がす

- [ ] **roof** 名屋根 (のようなもの)
- [ ] **room** 熟 run out of a room 部屋から駆け出して行く
- [ ] **rope** 名綱, なわ, ロープ
- [ ] **row** 名 (横に並んだ) 列 a row of 1列の〜
- [ ] **rude** 形粗野な, 無作法な, 失礼な
- [ ] **run** 熟 come running 飛んでくる, かけつける run around 走り回る run away 走り去る, 逃げ出す run into 〜に駆け込む, 〜の中に走って入る run out of 〜から駆け出す run out of a room 部屋から駆け出して行く run straight for 〜へまっしぐらに走る
- [ ] **rush** 動突進する, せき立てる rush off 急いで出て行く

S

- [ ] **sadly** 副悲しそうに, 不幸にも
- [ ] **sadness** 名悲しみ, 悲哀
- [ ] **safety** 名安全, 無事
- [ ] **salute** 動敬礼する
- [ ] **same** 熟 at the same time 同時に the same 〜 as … …と同じ (ような) 〜
- [ ] **sardine** 名イワシ
- [ ] **satyr** 名サテュロス《ヤギの脚をもつ半人半獣 (ギリシャ神話)》
- [ ] **saucer** 名受け皿
- [ ] **say unhappily** 浮かない顔をして言う
- [ ] **scared** 形おびえた, びっくりした be scared of 〜を恐れる
- [ ] **scary** 形恐ろしい, こわい, 臆病な
- [ ] **scent** 名①(快い) におい, 香り ②手がかり pick up a scent 匂いに気付く
- [ ] **scissors** 名はさみ
- [ ] **scratchy** 形チクチクする

- [ ] **scream** 動金切り声を出す
- [ ] **secret** 名秘密, 神秘 keep 〜 a secret from 〜を (人) に秘密にしておく
- [ ] **secretly** 副秘密に, 内緒で
- [ ] **see for oneself** 自分の目で確かめる
- [ ] **see if** 〜かどうかを確かめる
- [ ] **seek** 動捜し求める, 求める play hide and seek かくれんぼをして遊ぶ
- [ ] **seem** 動 (〜に) 見える, (〜のように) 思われる
- [ ] **send someone on** (人) を〜に送り出す
- [ ] **sense** 名①感覚, 感じ ②《-s》意識, 正気, 本性 ③常識, 分別, センス ④意味 make sense うなずける, 理にかなう
- [ ] **serious** 形①まじめな, 真剣な ②重大な, 深刻な, (病気などが) 重い get serious 真面目になる
- [ ] **seriously** 副①真剣に, まじめに ②重大に
- [ ] **serve** 動①仕える, 奉仕する ②(客の) 応対をする, 給仕する, 食事[飲み物] を出す
- [ ] **set things right** 状況を正常な状態にする
- [ ] **setting** 名〔月や太陽が〕沈むこと
- [ ] **sewing machine** ミシン
- [ ] **shake** 動振る, 揺れる, 揺さぶる, 震える shake someone's hand (人) の手を握る
- [ ] **shape** 動形づくる, 具体化する
- [ ] **shave** 動 (ひげ・顔を) そる, 削る
- [ ] **she-beaver** 名雌のビーバー
- [ ] **shelf** 名棚
- [ ] **shell** 名抜け殻
- [ ] **shield** 名盾, 防御物
- [ ] **shine** 動①光る, 輝く ②光らせる, 磨く shine in 〔光が〕差し込む

□ **shone** 動 shine（光る）の過去, 過去分詞

□ **shook** 動 shake（振る）の過去

□ **shout** 動 叫ぶ

□ **shut** 動 閉める, 閉じる　**shut up**（人）を黙らせる

□ **sick** 熟 **feel sick** 気分が悪い

□ **side** 名 側, 横, そば, 斜面　**on each side** それぞれの側に　**on the side of** ～を味方して　**one side** 片側

□ **sight** 熟 **come in sight** 見えてくる　**in sight** 視野に入って　**out of sight** 見えないところに

□ **sign** 熟 **make a sign to** ～するように合図する

□ **signal** 動 合図する 名 合図

□ **silence** 名 沈黙, 無言, 静寂

□ **silent** 形 ①無言の, 黙っている ②静かな, 音を立てない ③活動しない

□ **silk** 名 絹（布）, 生糸

□ **silly** 形 おろかな, 思慮のない

□ **singing** 動 sing（歌う）の現在分詞 形 歌う, さえずる

□ **Sire** 名 陛下

□ **sit on** ～の上にある, ～の上に乗る, ～の上に乗って動けないようにする　**sit on the throne** 王位に就く

□ **sit up** 起き上がる, 上半身を起こす

□ **slap** 動（平手, 平たいもので）ぴしゃりと打つ　**slap someone across the face**（人）の顔を平手打ちする 名 平手打ち

□ **sleep** 熟 **go to sleep** 寝る

□ **sleepy** 形 ①眠い, 眠そうな ②活気のない

□ **sleigh** 名（馬に引かせる）そり

□ **slide** 動 滑る, 滑らせる, 滑って行く, 滑走する

□ **slip** 動 滑る　**slip away** すり抜ける, こっそり去る, 静かに立ち去る

□ **slope** 名 坂, 斜面, 傾斜

□ **slow down** 速度を落とす

□ **slowly** 副 遅く, ゆっくり

□ **smash** 動 粉々に砕く

□ **smile at** ～に微笑みかける

□ **smoke** 名 煙, 煙状のもの

□ **smooth** 形 滑らかな, すべすべした

□ **snowflake** 名 雪片

□ **snow-topped** 形 雪をかぶった

□ **so** 熟 **and so** そこで, それだから, それで　**even so** たとえそうであっても　**or so** ～かそこらで　**so many** 非常に多くの　**so that** ～するために, それで, ～できるように　**so ～ that …** 非常に～なので…

□ **sock** 名 ソックス, 靴下

□ **soldier** 名 兵士, 兵卒

□ **solid** 形 ①固体［固形］の ②頑丈な

□ **some more** もう少し

□ **some time** いつか, そのうち

□ **someday** 副 いつか, そのうち

□ **someone** 代 ある人, 誰か

□ **something** 代 ①ある物, 何か ②いくぶん, 多少

□ **sometimes** 副 時々, 時たま

□ **soon** 熟 **as soon as** ～するとすぐ, ～するや否や

□ **sound** 動 ～に聞こえる　**sound like** ～のように聞こえる

□ **space** 動 間隔を空ける

□ **sparkling** 形 ①輝く, きらめく, 火花を出す ②活気のある, 生き生きした ③発泡性の

□ **speak of** ～を口にする

□ **spell** 名（呪文の）魔力

□ **spirit** 名 ①精神, 気力 ②精霊　**high spirit** 不屈の精神

□ **spit** 動 吐く, つばを吐く　**spit on** ～に唾を吐きかける

□ **splash** 動（水・泥を）はね飛ばす

131

A
B
C
D
E
F
G
H
I
J
K
L
M
N
O
P
Q
R
S
T
U
V
W
X
Y
Z

□ **split** 動裂く, 裂ける, 割る, 割れる, 分裂させる［する］ **split into two pieces** 二つに分割される

□ **spot** 名①地点, 場所, 立場 ②斑点, しみ

□ **squirrel** 名リス

□ **stand by** そばに立つ, 傍観する, 待機する

□ **stand up** 立ち上がる

□ **stare** 動じっと［じろじろ］見る **stare at** ～をじっと見つめる

□ **start doing** ～し始める

□ **start off** 出発する

□ **statue** 名像

□ **stay hidden** 隠れたままでいる

□ **stay out of the way** ちょっかいを出さない

□ **step** 熟 **make a false step** 足を踏み外す **step out into** ～に踏み出す, ～に出ていく **step out of** ～から出る **step over** またぐ **take a few steps forward** 数歩前に出る **watch one's step** 足元に気をつける

□ **stick** 名棒, 杖 動①（突き）刺さる, 刺す ②くっつく, くっつける ③突き出る **stick ～ into** ～を…に突っ込む

□ **still** 形じっとした, 動かない

□ **stone** 名石, 小石

□ **stool** 名［椅子の］スツール

□ **stop doing** ～するのをやめる

□ **story** 熟 **make up a story** 作り話をする

□ **stove** 名①レンジ, こんろ ②ストーブ

□ **straight** 熟 **run straight for** ～へまっしぐらに走る

□ **strange-looking** 形外観［外見］が奇妙な

□ **strangely** 副奇妙に, 変に, 不思議なことに, 不慣れに **look strangely at** 怪訝な顔で～を見る

□ **stream** 名小川, 流れ

□ **stuck** stick（刺さる, くっつく, 突き出る）の過去, 過去分詞

□ **study** 名書斎

□ **stupid** 形ばかな, ばかげた

□ **subject** 名主題, 話題

□ **such a** そのような

□ **sudden** 形突然の, 急な

□ **suggest** 動～を提案する

□ **suit** 名①スーツ, 背広 ②ひとそろい, 一組 **suit of armor** 鎧一式

□ **sunlight** 名陽の当たるところ

□ **sunshine** 名日光

□ **supporter** 名サポーター, 支持者

□ **suppose** 動〔～だと〕思う

□ **surely** 副確かに, きっと

□ **surprised** 形驚いた **be surprised to do** ～して驚く

□ **surprising** 形驚くべき, 意外な

□ **Susan** 名スーザン《キャラクター名》

□ **sweaty** 形汗びっしょりの, 汗をかいた **get a bit sweaty** 少し汗ばむ

□ **swimming** 動swim（泳ぐ）の現在分詞 名水泳

□ **swing** 動①揺り動かす, 揺れる ②回転する, ぐるっと回す 名①揺れ, 振ること, 振動 ②ぶらんこ

□ **sword** 名①剣, 刀 ②武力

□ **swung** 動swing（揺れる）の過去, 過去分詞

T

□ **tail** 名尾, しっぽ

□ **take** 熟 **It takes someone ～ to** …（人）が…するのに～（時間など）がかかる **take a few steps forward** 数歩前に出る **take away** ①連れ去る ②取り上げる, 奪い去る ③取り除く

take back ①取り戻す ②（言葉，約束を）取り消す，撤回する **take care of** ~の世話をする，~の面倒を見る，~に対処する **take off**（衣服を）脱ぐ，取り去る，~を取り除く **take over** 引き継ぐ，支配する，乗っ取る **take someone away**（人）を連れ出す **take someone prisoner**（人）を人質に取る

□ **tale** 名話，物語 **fairy tale** おとぎ話

□ **tea things** 茶道具

□ **teacup** 名ティーカップ

□ **teapot** 名ティーポット，急須

□ **tear at** ~を引き裂こうとする

□ **tease** 動からかう

□ **tell a lie** うそをつく

□ **tell ~ how to ...** ~に…のやり方を教える

□ **tell ~ to ...** ~に…するように言う

□ **tent** 名テント，天幕

□ **terrible** 形ひどく悪い

□ **terribly** 副ひどく

□ **terrified** 形おびえた，こわがった

□ **thank ~ for** ~に対して礼を言う

□ **that** 熟 **after that** その後 **now that** 今や~だから，~からには **so that** ~するために，それで，~できるように **so ~ that** ~非常に~なので… **That's all right.** いいんですよ。

□ **then** 熟 **by then** その時までに **just then** そのとたんに

□ **there** 熟 **get there** そこに到着する，目的を達成する，成功する **over there** あそこに

□ **thick** 形密集した

□ **think of** ~のことを考える，~を思いつく，考え出す

□ **thirsty** 形①のどが渇いた ②渇望する

□ **this** 熟 **at this** これを見て，そこで

（すぐに）**by this time** この時までに，もうすでに **in this way** このようにして **like this** このような，こんなふうに **this one** これ，こちら

□ **those who** ~する人々

□ **though** 接①~にもかかわらず，~だが ②たとえ~でも **even though** ~であるけれども，~にもかかわらず

□ **throat** 名のど，気管

□ **throne** 名王座，王権 **sit on the throne** 王位に就く

□ **through** 熟 **all the way through** 十分に，すべて **come through** 通り抜ける，成功する，期待に沿う **go through** 通り抜ける，一つずつ順番に検討する **push one's way through** ~を押し分けて進む

□ **throughout** 前①~中，~を通じて ②~のいたるところに

□ **tie** 動縛る **tie up** ひもで縛る，縛り上げる，つなぐ，拘束する，提携させる

□ **tight** 形堅い，きつい，ぴんと張った 副堅く，しっかりと

□ **time** 熟 **all the time** ずっと，いつも，その間ずっと **any time** いつでも **at the same time** 同時に **by the time** ~する時までに **by this time** この時までに，もうすでに **every time** ~するときはいつも **for a long time** 長い間 **next time** 次回に **some time** いつか，そのうち **whole time** 始終

□ **tired** 形①疲れた，くたびれた ②あきた，うんざりした **get tired** 疲れる

□ **tiredness** 名疲労，倦怠

□ **title** 名題名，タイトル

□ **toast** 名①トースト ②乾杯

□ **together** 熟 **all together** みんなが一緒になって

□ **too much** 過度の

□ **too ~ to ...** …するには~すぎる

133

- □ **tool** 名 道具, 用具, 工具
- □ **top** 熟 on top of ～の上(部)に
- □ **touch** 動 当たる, 触れる
- □ **tour** 名 ツアー, 見て回ること, 視察
- □ **toward** 熟 point toward ～の方を指さす
- □ **track** 名 通った跡
- □ **train line** (鉄道の)路線
- □ **traitor** 名 反逆者, 裏切り者
- □ **tray** 名 盆, 盛り皿
- □ **treason** 名 裏切り[反逆]行為, 背信 high treason (国家や君主に対する反逆, 大逆)
- □ **tree-women** 名 木の妖精たち
- □ **tried** 動 try (試みる)の過去, 過去分詞
- □ **triumph** 名 (大)勝利, 大成功, 勝利の喜び
- □ **trouble** 熟 get in trouble 厄介ごと[トラブル・面倒なこと]に巻き込まれる in trouble 面倒な状況で, 困って
- □ **true** 熟 come true 実現する make someone's wish come true (人)の望みをかなえる
- □ **truly** 副 ①全く, 本当に, 真に ②心から, 誠実に
- □ **trumpet** 名 トランペット
- □ **trust** 動 信用[信頼]する, 委託する
- □ **truth** 名 ①真理, 事実, 本当 ②誠実, 忠実さ
- □ **truthful** 形 正直な, 真実の
- □ **Tumnus** 名 タムナス《キャラクター名》
- □ **Turkish delight** ロクム《トルコの伝統菓子, 粉砂糖をまぶしたゼリーあめ》
- □ **turn around** 振り向く, 向きを変える, 方向転換する
- □ **turn back** 元に戻る
- □ **turn into** ～に変わる
- □ **turn to** ～の方を向く, ～に頼る, ～に変わる
- □ **twice as good as** ～の2倍もよい

U

- □ **ugh** 間 うえっ, げっ《嫌悪・恐怖を表す》, こんこん《せきの音》, ぶーぶー《不平を表す》
- □ **uh** 間 あー, えー, ええと, そのー《ためらい》
- □ **undone** 動 undo (ほどく)の過去分詞
- □ **unhappily** 副 不幸に, 運悪く, 不愉快そうに say unhappily 浮かない顔をして言う
- □ **unhappy** 形 不運な, 不幸な
- □ **unicorn** 名 一角獣, ユニコーン
- □ **unless** 接 もし～でなければ, ～しなければ
- □ **unsure** 形 確かでない, 自信がない
- □ **untie** 動 ほどく, 解放する
- □ **unusual** 形 普通でない, 珍しい, 見[聞き]慣れない
- □ **up** 熟 climb up onto ～の上に登る come up 近づいてくる, 階上に行く, 浮上する, 水面へ上ってくる, 発生する, 芽を出す get up 起き上がる, 立ち上がる give up あきらめる, やめる, 引き渡す grow up 成長する, 大人になる hold up ～を持ち上げる jump up 素く立ち上がる look up 見上げる look up to ～を仰ぎ見る make up 作り出す, ～を構成[形成]する make up a story 作り話をする pick up 拾い上げる pick up a scent 匂いに気付く pull up 引っ張り上げる put up ～を上げる shut up (人)を黙らせる sit up 起き上がる, 上半身を起こす stand up 立ち上がる tie up ひもで縛る, 縛り上げる, つなぐ, 拘束する, 提携させる up to ～まで, ～に

至るまで，～に匹敵して **up to now** 今まで **wake up** 起きる，目を覚ます **walk up** 歩み寄る，歩いて上る **walk up to** ～に歩み寄る **warm oneself up** 体を温める **warm up** 暖まる，温める，ウォーミングアップする，盛り上がる

□ **upon** 前 ①《場所・接触》～（の上）に ②《日・時》～に ③《関係・従事》～に関して，～について，～して

□ **upset** 形腹を立てて **make someone upset**（人）を動揺させる

□ **upsetting** 形動揺させるような

□ **used** 動 use（使う）の過去，過去分詞 形慣れている，《be－to》～に慣れてくる

V

□ **valley** 名谷，渓谷

□ **very** 熟 **The very idea!** とんでもない！ **very well** 結構，よろしい

□ **visitor** 名訪問者，観光客

W

□ **wait** 熟 **can't wait to** ～したくてたまらない **wait for** ～を待つ

□ **waiting** 動 they（待つ）の現在分詞 名待機

□ **wake up** 起きる，目を覚ます

□ **walk** 熟 **walk across** ～を歩いて渡る **walk around** 歩き回る，ぶらぶら歩く **walk away** 立ち去る，遠ざかる **walk on** 歩き続ける **walk over** ～の方に歩いていく **walk past** 通り過ぎる **walk to** ～まで歩いて行く **walk up** 歩み寄る，歩いて上る **walk up to** ～に歩み寄る

□ **wand** 名〔魔法の〕棒

□ **War Drobe** wardrobe（ワードローブ）の聞き間違い

□ **wardrobe** 名洋服だんす，ワードローブ

□ **warm up** 暖まる，温める，ウォーミングアップする，盛り上がる **warm oneself up** 体を温める

□ **watch one's step** 足元に気をつける

□ **waterfall** 名滝

□ **wave** 動振る

□ **way** 熟 **all the way** ずっと，はるばる，最後まで **all the way through** 十分に，すべて **find one's way back** 元の場所にたどり着く **in a different way** 別の方法で **in a kind way** 優しく **in this way** このようにして **long way** はるかに **most of the way** ほとんど **on one's way**〔目的地への〕途中にいる **push one's way through** ～を押し分けて進む **stay out of the way** ちょっかいを出さない **way to** ～する方法

□ **weapon** 名武器

□ **week** 熟 **following week** 翌週

□ **well** 熟 **very well** 結構，よろしい **well done** うまくやった

□ **wet** 形ぬれた，湿った，雨の

□ **what** 熟 **no matter what** たとえどんな～であろうと **what about** ～についてはどうですか **what if** もし～だったらどうなるだろうか **what … for** どんな目的で **What's the matter?** どうしたんですか

□ **where to go** 行くべき所

□ **wherever** 接どこでも，どこへ［で］～するとも

□ **while** 熟 **for a while** しばらくの間，少しの間

□ **whip** 名むち

□ **whisker** 名〔猫やネズミの〕ひげ

□ **whisper** 動ささやく，小声で話す 名ささやき，ひそひそ話，うわさ

□ **White Witch** 白の魔女

□ **who** 熟 those who ~する人々

□ **whoever** 代 ~する人は誰でも，誰が~しようとも

□ **whole** 形 全体の，すべての，完全な，満~，丸~ whole time 始終

□ **whom** 代 ①誰を［に］②《関係代名詞》~するところの人，そしてその人を

□ **wide** 形 幅の広い，広範囲の，幅が~ある 副 広く，大きく開いて

□ **will have done** ~してしまっているだろう《未来完了形》

□ **wine** 名 ワイン，ぶどう酒

□ **wing** 名 翼，羽

□ **wipe** 動 ~をふく，ぬぐう，ふきとる wipe ~ away ~を拭い取る

□ **wish** 熟 make someone's wish come true (人) の望みをかなえる

□ **witch** 名 魔法使い，魔女 White Witch 白の魔女

□ **with** 熟 agree with (人) に同意する along with ~と一緒に be covered with ~でおおわれている be filled with ~でいっぱいになる delighted with ~を喜んでいる go along with ~に同調する go with ~と一緒に行く help ~ with …… を~の面で手伝う look at someone with awe 感心したように (人) の顔を見る make friends with ~と友達になる with a laugh 笑いながら with hard eyes 厳しい目つきで with plenty of たくさんの~

□ **without** 熟 can't live without ~ なしで生きられない not … without ~ing ~せずには…しない，~すれば必ず…する

□ **woken** 動 wake (目が覚める) の過去分詞

□ **wolf** 名 オオカミ (狼)

□ **wolfkiller** 名 狼殺し

□ **wolves** 名 wolf (オオカミ) の複数

□ **wonder** 動 ①不思議に思う，(~に) 驚く ②(~かしらと) 思う wonder if ~ではないかと思う

□ **word** 熟 my word これは驚いた

□ **work** 熟 go to work 仕事に取りかかる

□ **world** 熟 in all parts of the world 全世界の地域で in the world 世界で

□ **worry about** ~のことを心配する be worried about (~のことで) 心配している，~が気になる［かかる］

□ **worse** 形 いっそう悪い，より劣った，よりひどい get worse 悪化する 副 いっそう悪く

□ **Would you like ~?** ~はいかがですか。

□ **would like to** ~したいと思う

□ **write to** ~に手紙を書く

Y

□ **year** 熟 for ~ years ~年間，~年にわたって

□ **yell** 動 大声を上げる，怒鳴る

□ **your Majesty** 陛下

□ **yummy** 形 おいしい

Z

□ **zoo** 名 動物園

English Conversational Ability Test
国際英語会話能力検定

● E-CATとは…
英語が話せるようになるための
テストです。インターネット
ベースで、30分であなたの発
話力をチェックします。

www.ecatexam.com

● iTEP®とは…
世界各国の企業、政府機関、アメリカの大学
300校以上が、英語能力判定テストとして採用。
オンラインによる90分のテストで文法、リー
ディング、リスニング、ライティング、スピー
キングの5技能をスコア化。iTEP®は、留学、就
職、海外赴任などに必要な、世界に通用する英
語力を総合的に評価する画期的なテストです。

www.itepexamjapan.com

ラダーシリーズ

The Chronicles of Narnia:
The Lion, the Witch and the Wardrobe ナルニア国物語 ライオンと魔女

2023年5月4日　第1刷発行

原著者　C. S. ルイス

発行者　浦　晋亮

発行所　**IBCパブリッシング株式会社**
　　　　〒162-0804 東京都新宿区中里町29番3号
　　　　菱秀神楽坂ビル
　　　　Tel. 03-3513-4511　Fax. 03-3513-4512
　　　　www.ibcpub.co.jp

© IBC Publishing, Inc. 2023

印　　刷　株式会社シナノパブリッシングプレス
装　　丁　伊藤 理恵
イラスト　高橋 玲奈

Printed in Japan
ISBN978-4-7946-0757-7